Miles Cowsill

Brittany Ferries

40 MEMORABLE YEARS

Published by: Ferry Publications, PO Box 33, Ramsey, Isle of Man, British Isles IM99 4LP

Tel: +44 (0) 1624 898445   Fax: +44 (0) 1624 898449   E-mail: ferrypubs@manx.net   Website: www.ferrypubs.co.uk

Contributors: Stephen Tuckwell
Christopher Jones
Gillian Thornton
Linda Cowsill
Trevor Barrett

The author of this book is grateful to all those who have contributed to the publication. A special word of thanks should go to the Directors of Brittany Ferries: Martine Jourdren (Group Managing Director and Chairman of the Executive Board), Christophe Mathieu (Group Strategy and Commercial Director) and Frédéric Pouget (Group Maritime Port and Operations Director), who have not only contributed but also assisted with the production of this publication. Thanks should also go to the following for their assistance with the book: Mike Louagie/ShipPax, Bruce Peter, Brian Smith, Gilles Quéré (Captain of the Pont-Aven*); Mario Stevelinck (Purser,* Bretagne*), Nigel Long, Kevin Mitchell and FotoFlite.*

Produced and designed by Ferry Publications trading as Lily Publications Ltd
PO Box 33, Ramsey, Isle of Man, British Isles, IM99 4LP.
Tel: +44 (0) 1624 898446   Fax: +44 (0) 1624 898449
www.ferrypubs.co.uk   e-mail: info@lilypublications.co.uk

Contents

Foreword

Like most of the farmers who each own a part of Brittany Ferries, I was a child when it was founded 40 years ago. Growing up in the farming community of Brittany and watching our ferry company flourish has given me a strong sense of attachment to it as well as a feeling of gratitude for the major part it has played in opening up and bringing wealth to the region. Brittany Ferries is more, much more, than a simple transporter of people and goods. It is an integral part of the economic infrastructure of Western France.

The story of how we started is now pretty widely known but to interpret this simply as a bunch of farmers having one bright idea and starting a ferry is to do the founders a great injustice. Brittany Ferries is but one element in a portfolio of developments we have undertaken and, as ferries have changed, so has farming. Both are capital intensive and highly risky, depending on many factors outside our control, such as exchange rates, consumer demand and even the weather. This has made us very resilient and suspicious of commonly-held views. We are essentially entrepreneurs who like to swim against the tide and take decisions based not on short-term expediency but on what is good for the company and the community in the long term.

Jean-Marc Roué

This is why we invest in original works of art for our ships (we have over 2000 pieces) in order to enrich our customers' experience. It is also why we operate under the French flag and employ French crew, so that our passengers' holidays start the moment they board, whilst most of our competitors use cheaper options.

For us quality cannot be compromised. Over 40 years we have built a strong image in the UK, our major market, and earned a well-deserved reputation for providing a high-quality service – which is why we enjoy levels of repeat business far above the industry norm. But with 80% of our earnings derived from the UK in sterling and most of our costs borne in euros (because of our French crews) and in dollars for fuel, it is easy to see how we suffer when the pound is weak. As in any other business, our response has been to improve efficiency and reduce costs but without any reduction in quality or choice of routes for our customers.

We have also embarked on an exciting new project with the shipbuilder STX to evaluate a new cruiseferry design powered by liquefied natural gas. This development is driven not only for reasons of economy but because we are committed to reducing emissions of both CO_2 and pollutants.

The past 40 years have seen Brittany Ferries grow from just one route and one freighter to a company linking Great Britain, Ireland, France and Spain with nine routes and a fleet of nine ships, many of which are luxury cruiseferries. However, our roots remain very firmly in Brittany and I, as a Breton farmer, am very proud to have the honour of leading this fine company into the next 40 years.

Jean-Marc Roué
President,
Brittany Ferries

Introduction

Forty years on from its creation in 1973, forward-looking Brittany Ferries is a company with immense pride in its history and heritage, and a real passion for perpetuating the obstinacy, entrepreneurial spirit and drive of its pioneering founders – a farming co-operative led by the late Alexis Gourvennec. And it is no coincidence that company President Jean-Marc Roué, who succeeded Gourvennec in the role, is himself a Breton farmer too.

From a single freight ship purchased for the sole purpose of transporting the co-operative's fresh produce to the markets of south-west England, Brittany Ferries has risen to the elite ranks of Europe's most successful and respected ferry operators. Business on the company's first route, Roscoff-Plymouth, grew rapidly and today there are nine routes – five between three ports in the UK and four ports in France, another between France and Ireland, and three longer routes between England and Spain. And in the process of establishing, developing and maintaining these services, Brittany Ferries has become a significant and integral component of the tourism industries of both France and Spain.

If there is one enduring quality above all others which has elevated Brittany Ferries to its current status, it is the passion to be different – not in the purely token sense expressed by so many advertisers desperate to stand out in today's ferociously competitive consumer markets, but in the real sense of not following the herd. For example, the company's stubborn refusal to buy the least expensive ships and employ the cheapest labour is apparent from the quality and modernity of the vessels in the fleet and the consistently high standards of courtesy and service to which passengers are treated. Indeed, the ships are much more akin to cruise liners than to the conventional notions and expectations of what ferries should look like and the facilities and service they should deliver. And Brittany Ferries' desire to be truly 'different' is evident in the personalisation of each ship, no two looking the same in external or interior design and each with its own unique onboard ambience. A clear illustration of this philosophy is the collection of original works of art displayed in the public areas, every piece individually commissioned from contemporary artists to satisfy a relevant theme. The most famous of these is the late Scottish artists Alexander Goudie.

This singular approach by Brittany Ferries means that in stark contrast to other ferry operators, not only are there no identical or 'sister' ships in the company's fleet; many regular passengers such as holiday home

owners, lorry drivers and holidaymakers form emotional bonds with a particular ship of their liking and this becomes an intrinsic part of the whole travel and/or holiday experience. The same ties apply to the officers and crew. Despite the company's rapid expansion since 1986, each crew still functions very much as a close-knit family unit.

Another factor in the success of Brittany Ferries is that as the vast majority of passengers are British, responsibility for the company's marketing lies on the English side of the Channel and the French take care of onboard services and operating the ships – a division of work which continues to work to everyone's advantage, particularly as on the comparatively long-haul services to Spain the ships are akin to floating hotels and, across the fleet as a whole, accommodation is all en suite and numbers almost 7,000 beds.

Significant and successful milestones in marketing have included the decision in 1978 to offer Brits affordable ferry-inclusive family holidays to France, the choice of holiday accommodation ranging from rural gites in the earliest days to hotels and grand châteaux later, with the further inclusion of Spain as a ferry-inclusive holiday destination. With the emphasis on quality, value for money and convenience – take your own car and pack everything you need – this concept in self-drive holidays proved to be an enduring hit which remains very popular today.

The growth too in Brits' second-home ownership in France and Spain has been advantageous to Brittany Ferries in helping to generate additional year-round passenger income, and these regular and loyal travellers have been rewarded with the benefits of their own dedicated Brittany Ferries club.

In 2005 came the company's first high-speed service. The acquisition of the giant InCat craft, *Normandie Express*, reduced the Portsmouth-Caen and Portsmouth-Cherbourg crossing times to just 210 and 180 minutes respectively.

2011 heralded the option of a second route to Spain, the destination port being the Basque city of Bilbao – a service which has further justified Brittany Ferries' investment in strengthening its market-leading status on the Western Channel.

My own first experience of travelling with Brittany Ferries came in 1976 on the *Penn ar Bed* (known at that time as the Penn no Bed because of her lack of cabins!) on the Plymouth-Roscoff route. For the whole of the 9-hour overnight sailing my student girlfriend and I endured the discomfort of aircraft seating – a far, far cry from the luxuriously-appointed cabins of today's fleet. But at least we managed to pool enough money to treat ourselves to dinner in the onboard restaurant prior to our camping holiday in Brittany. I still remember that the meal was outstanding yet very realistically priced, even on a student's budget. And it was a foretaste of the cuisine which was to set Brittany Ferries apart and become one of the pillars of the company's subsequent and enduring success.

Over the years since I've been privileged to sail on the majority of the 46 ships which the company has operated in its 40-year tenure, and to make friends with many of the people within Brittany Ferries, both on land and sea. I've been very fortunate to have access to such a remarkable story. And as the company

Penn Ar Bed *(Ferry Publications Library)*

sails into its fifth decade, there will be yet more challenges and hurdles to overcome, from regulations calculated to protect and preserve the environment to the cost of fuel, continued competition from low-cost airlines and the Channel Tunnel, and passengers' expectations of ever-better quality and choices of holiday destinations and accommodation.

Finally, I would like to express my thanks to all those who have contributed to this book, which I hope will give you a rare insight into a truly unique company – not only in terms of its history and day-to-day operation but also the future path in which the Breton directors are likely to take Brittany Ferries as it heads towards its next big birthday: the 50th anniversary!

Miles Cowsill - Isle of Man
March 2013

CHAPTER ONE

The man who made waves

It's hard to imagine a greater transformation in any working man's fortunes than that of rising from humble vegetable grower on a peasant farm in France to standing proudly (for 35 years) at the helm of an outrageously unlikely, groundbreaking and enduring French shipping line.

Yet such was the 'fairy-tale' life of Alexis Gourvennec. Born in Finistère, northern Brittany, on 11th January 1936, the son of a labourer and vegetable-growing smallholder, he left school at 14 and just ten years later, in 1961, he was the ringleader as thousands of farmers and their tractors descended on Morlaix in protest at the continuing injustice of struggling local vegetable growers being ripped off by greedy middlemen (a conflict referred to at the time as the 'artichoke wars').

Gourvennec was arrested – a very small price to pay for the radical reform which De Gaulle's government duly introduced, empowering farmers across France to create their own price-controlling marketing co-operatives. Gourvennec's co-operative, in a very productive agricultural area near Roscoff, subsequently became the country's most powerful.

This reform was only the beginning of Gourvennec's vision to stimulate regional growth and to sell to markets beyond the confines of Brittany's borders. For too long, the region's fortunes had been in the hands of out-of-touch decision-makers in Paris – a strangehold he was determined to break.

His fire, passion and ability to kick up a storm to produce results were recognised and harnessed by local politicians, and persistent lobbying in Paris by the development board for western Brittany, created by Gourvennec, finally persuaded ministers to release the purse strings and authorise substantial government investment in developing the region's infrastructure. Result: the creation of new roads and other vital amenities, most significantly a deep-water port at Roscoff.

Along with Britain's decision to join the EEC, the port presented Gourvennec and his co-operative with the big opportunity they craved – a whole new market for their fresh produce across the Channel. Plymouth and south-west England beckoned. All that was needed was the shipping line to deliver the goods.

But when presented with the co-operative's proposition, the existing ferry operators poured cold water over the notion that such an enterprise could ever pay its way, let alone make money. Gourvennec's response was true to his nature: if *you* won't do it, *we* will. And they did. The company which is today Brittany Ferries was born.

By introducing a daily ferry service to Plymouth from Roscoff, the co-operative had complete control over the export of its own produce. Moreover, the enterprise was such a success that in time other cross-Channel routes followed – Roscoff-Cork, St Malo-Portsmouth and Santander-Plymouth. And not only did the company prosper – it became the first French shipping line to carry passengers and freight traffic.

Alexis Gourvennec was one of those people born to succeed. Amongst his other achievements was that of pig-breeding tycoon, his pig farm becoming one of the biggest in Europe.

For a man who left school at the age of 14, his achievements could only be described as remarkable. And even he was amazed at the success of Brittany Ferries. In 2006, when he was president of the company, he wrote: "Who would have thought that Brittany Ferries would become the major force in tourism that it undoubtedly is today?"

Alexis Gourvennec died in Morlaix in February 2007 at the age of 71.

Alexis Gourvennec on his farm at Morlaix. *(Brittany Ferries)*

Alexis Gourvennec, Christian Michielini, Maurice Chollet and Prince Charles at Roscoff for development of relations between Britain and Cornwall. *(Brittany Ferries)*

CHAPTER TWO

From the land to the sea

In 1964 British Rail closed its St Malo-Southampton service, the *St. Patrick* making her last sailing to the Hampshire port on 27th September. BR's reasoning for the termination was that it could not make the operation pay its way. And although it was fact that in the ship's last season there were fewer than 100 passengers on most sailings, and cargo loadings were dismally poor too – less than 800 tons for the whole year – it can also be justly claimed that these statistics were the direct result of British Rail's failure to actively promote and market the service on either side of the Channel, and its demise was therefore as predictable as it was inevitable. The same was true of the BR cross-Channel Le Havre and Cherbourg services, which also ceased in 1964.

For Breton vegetable farmers in particular, including Alexis Gourvennec's influential co-operative, the consequences of BR's St Malo-Southampton termination were a body blow. Thoresen Car Ferries subsequently took over from BR and reopened the Le Havre and Cherbourg routes, but both were a far from satisfactory compromise for the Brittany farmers as the longer distances and sailing times involved between these Normandy ports and England's south coast were not suited to transporting fresh produce. Equally, the costs were greater too – prohibitive, in fact. There had to be a better solution.

When that solution was announced, it came from the farming co-operative itself, led by Alexis Gourvennec, and it stunned the shipping world by declaring that it would finance and operate its own ferry services. On paper at least, it made perfect sense, giving farmers in the co-operative total control over their own destiny. The established ferry operators saw things differently, pouring scorn on the idea that vegetable-growing Breton upstarts could successfully turn their novice hands to all the complexities of running and maintaining a viable shipping line. But undeterred, and with their feet firmly on the ground, Alexis Gourvennec and his associates pressed ahead. Their new enterprise, which they called Brittany Ferries, became a startling and very ambitious reality.

To operate its innovative cross-Channel link, new kid on the block Brittany Ferries opted to sail between western Brittany – specifically, the pretty fishing town and port of Roscoff – and historic Plymouth in Devon. It would not be the first time that the two towns had traded with each other; since the early 19th century, onion growers from Roscoff (who in time came to be known as Onion Johnnies) had made an annual pilgrimage to sell their strings of prized and famous pink onions not only in Plymouth but all over England – an enterprise immortalised in Roscoff's Onion Johnnies Museum and within smaller aspects of the town's architectural detail.

However, before the new Brittany Ferries service could get under way, major construction work was necessary as neither Plymouth nor Roscoff were suitably equipped for ferry operation. At Roscoff the requirement was a new deep-water harbour, 3 km from the town centre, and huge quantities of rock were moved to provide the quays and facilities. Work was completed in September 1972 at a cost of some 17 million francs.

In Plymouth, the British Transport Docks Board awarded a £400,000 contract to Thomas & Co. Ltd. to build a 180-foot linkspan at the Millbay Docks so that loading and unloading would be possible at all states of the tide. To facilitate the linkspan, dredging work was essential. Furthermore, a two-acre area of land was earmarked for marshalling yards and provision also made for an additional four acres for the terminal's future development.

Under the leadership of Alexis Gourvennec, Brittany Ferries' initial plans were focused entirely on offering and promoting a freight-only service, and the purchase of the ro-ro ship *Lilac* (2,293 gross tons and with deck capacity for 45 lorries) fitted the bill. On 17th December 1972, Madame Annie Gourvennec aptly renamed the ship *Kerisnel*, after a small village in

Above: **Kerisnel** *(Ferry Publications Library)*

Left: Roscoff 1973. *(Ferry Publications Library)*

The first crew of **Kerisnel**, Francis Jan, Chief Engineer, Commandant Ernest Lainé and Gérard Le Saux, Second Captain. (*Brittany Ferries*)

The gift and duty-free shop on the **Penn Ar Bed**. (*Brittany Ferries*)

The inauguration of the **Kerisnel** on 18th December 1972. (*Brittany Ferries*)

Brittany renowned for its cauliflowers. Prior to entering service with Brittany Ferries, the *Kerisnel* had been on charter to P&O Normandy Ferries to cover for refits of its vessels on the Southampton-Le Havre route.

THE STORY SO FAR: 40 MEMORABLE YEARS

1973

On 1st January, with a choir singing carols and French, British and Breton flags flying, the bold enterprise known as Brittany Ferries was officially born. Almost 3,000 people attended the opening of the terminal at Roscoff on this otherwise bleak New Year's Day, and a spokesman announced that the company aimed to convey around 150,000 tons of cargo during its first year.

The *Kerisnel* duly set sail on the new service's inaugural Channel crossing, arriving at Plymouth on the morning of the 3rd. First to disembark was 28-year-old Jean Claude Rolland, his lorry loaded with apples,

cauliflowers, Corsican wine and cigarette papers. At this early stage Brittany Ferries had envisaged three sailings a week in each direction, increasing to five at the height of the produce season to meet the anticipated demand of freight hauliers, and expected to carry around 40,000 tons of traffic in the first three months. But it was soon disappointed: the actual figure was just 17,000 – a fact tempered by the realisation that any new service needs time to gather momentum.

It was also quickly apparent from the launch of this new freight-only Roscoff-Plymouth service that there was demand too for a passenger service, Brittany emerging as a popular destination for British tourists. Consequently, Brittany Ferries and Vedettes Armoricaines of Brest jointly agreed to operate a passenger-only service using the *Poseidon* (1,358 gross tons), a former day-only Baltic vessel of Stena Line. Launch date was set for 5th April 1973 but due to contractual disagreements on both sides of the

Penn Ar Bed *(Ferry Publications Library)*

Channel it was delayed until 19th May, sailing initially from Plymouth's Trinity Pier to the Roscoff ferry terminal on Mondays, Tuesdays and Fridays.

Again, the new service had a somewhat shaky start and was erratic to say the least. On occasion the *Poseidon* did not sail to England, the company claiming lack of passengers. But things settled down and during July the *Poseidon* averaged 120 passengers a day, finishing her maiden 1973 summer season on 15th September.

Whilst this trial passenger service was operating, Brittany Ferries placed an order with a shipyard at La Rochelle in France to build an enterprising new ferry for this Plymouth-Roscoff service – a ship designed to carry passengers, their cars and freight.

Other significant events in 1973, the year of Brittany Ferries' birth? These included the introduction of VAT in the UK, Richard Nixon's infamous Watergate scandal, the end of the war in Vietnam, and Plymouth Argyle's 3-2 victory over Pele and his Brazilian team Santos at Home Park!

1974

The completion of the new Brittany Ferries ship (named *Penn Ar Bed* – Breton for Land's End) was delayed and she was unable to undergo sea trials until mid-January 1974. It was shortly before midnight on 24th January that the *Penn Ar Bed* (2,891 gross tons), under the command of Captain Ernest Laine, slipped her moorings at Roscoff on her maiden voyage to Plymouth.

Above: **Armorique**
(FotoFlite)

Right: **Prince of Brittany** (Ferry Publications Library)

Left: **Cornouailles** (Ferry Publications Library)

In the light of good bookings for the following season, Brittany Ferries produced its first glossy brochure – a page-turning, high-quality publication which set the benchmark for the ferry industry. This and other subsequent Brittany Ferries brochures played no small part in creating a much greater awareness of the attractions awaiting British holidaymakers in beautiful neighbouring Brittany.

1975

During January, Christian Michielini joined Brittany Ferries as Managing Director and over the following two decades was to play a substantial role in the company's success and growth.

One initiative was to explore the potential benefits of introducing another ferry route from Brittany to England. As a late-summer experiment to test its viability, three sailings a week were made from St Malo to Plymouth in the period mid-August to early October.

1976

The trial proved a great success, resulting in a new service linking St Malo and the newly-established ferry port at Portsmouth. The ship chosen to operate it was the French-built *Terje Vigen* (5,732 gross tons), originally built to serve between Norway and Denmark. Norwegian registered, she was purchased by Brittany Ferries and underwent a major refit prior to her arrival at Plymouth on 4th March. Renamed the *Armorique*, she opened the St Malo-Portsmouth service on 17th June.

With two ferry links from Brittany to England and three ships, Brittany Ferries now looked poised to break new records, and such was the company's confidence that it ordered a new ship from a Norwegian yard for delivery the following season.

1977

The newly-built *Cornouailles* (3,383 gross tons) entered service on 24th May 1977 and sailings between Roscoff and Plymouth were increased, with up to three a day at weekends. This was a very successful year too for the *Armorique* on the St Malo-Portsmouth route, with increased passenger traffic on the link.

In autumn, Brittany Ferries announced further expansion plans for 1978, notably new services from England to Spain and from Roscoff to Cork. There was nothing new in the idea of a British-Spanish link; during the previous ten years three other lines had served Spain from Southampton. But Brittany Ferries opted to sail from Plymouth, believing that it offered passengers a shorter and more convenient crossing time, and with the French government's consent to allow the company's ships to sail close to Brittany's western coast, sailings each way were reduced to 23 hours compared with the two nights at sea which had been the downfall of previous operators.

The new twice-weekly service was to be operated by the *Armorique*, departing from Plymouth on Monday and Wednesday and returning on Wednesday and Friday, thereby providing an extra sailing on the Roscoff route and enabling her to make a round trip to Cork at the weekends. To prepare her for these new and longer schedules she underwent a major refit, her

Quiberon *(Ferry Publications Library)*

Quiberon *(Ferry Publications Library)*

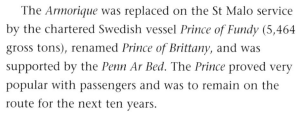

novel attractions including a cinema, playroom and improved catering facilities.

1978

The *Armorique* was replaced on the St Malo service by the chartered Swedish vessel *Prince of Fundy* (5,464 gross tons), renamed *Prince of Brittany*, and was supported by the *Penn Ar Bed*. The *Prince* proved very popular with passengers and was to remain on the route for the next ten years.

On 17th April, the *Armorique* opened the new Plymouth-Santander link and also quickly found favour with passengers, the service extended in 1979 to operate all year round. Over the next ten years demand grew very rapidly, creating the need for larger tonnage. The

new seasonal Irish service was a similar success.

1979

Boosted by encouraging signs of increased passenger and car traffic, Brittany Ferries looked forward to the next season with great confidence. But in the event it was fraught with problems, overcome by chartering a variety of vessels to maintain operations.

1980

Three vessels duly entered service for the season, the company chartering the Italian freight ship *Faraday* (2,932 gross tons) to cover freight operations on the St. Malo route, and purchasing the 10-year-old Greek freight ship *Iniochos Express* (2,768 gross tons) from Iniochos

Goëlo *(FotoFlite)*

Shipping S.A. to cover the Plymouth-Santander and Roscoff operations. Built in Hong Kong for the Union S.S. Co., New Zealand, she was renamed *Breizh-Izel*.

Meanwhile, with bookings achieving an encouraging high, the summer passenger schedules for the St Malo-Portsmouth route were extended and the Finnish vessel *Viking 6* (5,073 gross tons and renamed *Goëlo*, a region in north-east Brittany) was chartered to operate on the 9-hour link for the next two seasons. 1980 also saw the purchase of the *Prince of Brittany* from her Swedish owners for $8 million.

The year was progressing well until mid-August, when all services were disrupted by industrial action as disgruntled French fishermen blockaded the Channel ports. Trouble flared on the 'unlucky' 13th as the first

of the ports was affected, and within a week the dispute worsened and all French ferry ports were closed. On 20th August, at around 90-minute intervals, the *Armorique*, *Prince of Brittany* and *Goëlo* sailed from Plymouth to Spain, taking stranded holidaymakers on the 23-hour trip. The *Penn Ar Bed* set sail the next day.

The industrial action thus committed Brittany Ferries to considerable extra expense. Not only did the dispute close the company's ports but also meant that the crews on the French ships were unable to change over. But then, on 21st August, the Brittany Ferries ship the *Cornouailles* broke the blockade at Roscoff and by the end of that week the drama was over, the French fishermen agreeing to reopen the blockaded ports to holiday traffic.

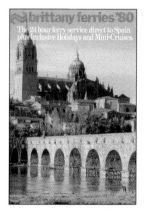

During December Brittany Ferries announced plans to charter the Fred. Olsen ship *Bolero* (11,344 gross tons and to be renamed *Trégor*) to expand and improve the Santander route by increasing to three sailings to Spain a week. But at the eleventh hour the deal collapsed as it could not be finalised in time for the 1981 season. Meanwhile, traffic figures for 1980 were up again on the previous year by an impressive 18%, due in part to the choice of attractive package holidays in France which Brittany Ferries were now offering. But the picture didn't look quite so rosy when the company disclosed a trading loss for the year of £1 million.

1981

In autumn, further financial problems came to light as Brittany Ferries announced that losses for 1981 would be in the region of £2.4 million – the result of heavy borrowing for the purchase of new tonnage, and to a lesser extent created by the price war which for the last two years had raged between rival ferry operators on the English Channel. To overcome the difficulties, measures were taken to consolidate the company's position, notably a reorganisation of the Group's structure.

Within the following 10 years, Brittany Ferries was to develop into not only the biggest ferry company in the western sector of the English Channel but also the proud operator of the Channel's most modern fleet.

1982

With Brittany Ferries back on a firm financial footing, further expansion and development rapidly took place. Demand on all of the company's routes increased and for the Santander service in particular, resulting in the charter (with the option to buy) of the 1975 German-built ship *Nils Dacke* (7,950 gross tons). Able to operate at 22.5 knots, she could if required reduce the crossing time to Spain by some two hours during peak season. She was renamed *Quiberon*, after the peninsula and town in southern Brittany, and an extensive refit included alterations to her car decks to provide extra cabins, increasing her capacity to 1,040 passengers and 252 cars. The *Quiberon* entered service in May, allowing the *Armorique* to return to the St. Malo-Portsmouth link which she inaugurated in 1976.

1983

Brittany Ferries, born out of the need to transport fresh farm produce to England, celebrated its tenth birthday at the turn of the year and by now boasted a fleet of six ships and four ferry routes. And in the coming ten years the growth of the company was to prove even more dramatic.

In readiness for the summer season, more than £1 million was spent upgrading the passenger facilities on the *Quiberon*, *Prince of Brittany* and *Armorique*. The summer schedules were similar to those of the previous year, but during the season's peak time the freight ship *Breizh-Izel* was introduced on the Santander route to support the *Quiberon*.

This year also saw the successful charter of the Danish- registered *Gelting Nord* (4,371 gross tons) for the Roscoff-Plymouth service, replacing the *Cornouailles*. Renamed *Bénodet* after the resort in southern Brittany, she entered service on 30th April and was a major improvement, offering more space for cars and better cabin and passenger accommodation than did her predecessor.

1984

Early in the new year, Jersey's government made it known that they were looking for another operator to compete with Sealink on the Channel Islands services from mainland Britain. By spring, a consortium of Brittany Ferries, Jersey-based Huelin-Renouf and the haulage company Mainland Market Deliveries (MMD) was considering plans to grasp the opportunity by utilising the sale-listed *Penn Ar Bed*. But she proved unsuitable for the service, the Department of Trade seeking a reduction in her freight capacity under the British flag. The *Penn Ar Bed* was consequently sold to Swedish interests and the search was on for a likely alternative.

By the end of the year, Huelin-Renouf announced that with the backing of Brittany Ferries (27% interest) and MMD (the principal haulage company to the Channel Islands), the rival ferry service would start from March 1985 – news unlikely to be welcomed by Sealink British Ferries, who had held the monopoly of the Channel Islands services for most of the century.

The ship opening the new service, on 28th March 1985, would be the *Bénodet* (chartered to Brittany Ferries in 1983 for the Roscoff route and to be renamed *Corbière*), manned by a British crew.

At the end of 1984, following two very successful seasons on the Santander/Cork services, Brittany Ferries purchased the *Quiberon*, and with the *Bénodet* now required on the new Channel Islands link the

Top: **Bénodet** *(FotoFlite)*

Middle: **Breizh-Izel** *(FotoFlite)*

Below: **Prince of Brittany** *(FotoFlite)*

Above: **Duc de Normandie** leaving Caen. *(Miles Cowsill)*

Right: **Reine Mathilde** *(Miles Cowsill)*

company also initiated a 3-year bareboat charter of the Yugoslav ferry *Njegos* (3,998 gross tons). Renamed the *Trégastel*, she would enter service on the Roscoff-Plymouth service on 1st May 1985.

1985

During the summer of 1985, in the space of less than a month, Brittany Ferries announced that it had purchased the Dutch ferry *Prinses Beatrix* from SMZ (the Zeeland Steamship Company – the Dutch partner in Sealink operations) for a new service between Portsmouth and Lower Normandy. This was followed by the further news that Brittany Ferries had acquired the successful freight shipping company Truckline, freight-only operators between Poole and Cherbourg – a purchase which included Truckline's two ships and was a major boost to business.

For some time, following the decision by Portsmouth rivals Townsend Thoresen not to open a new ferry service to the port of Ouistreham (north of Caen), Brittany Ferries had also been contemplating the introduction of a new Portsmouth-Normandy link and was offered the port – an opportunity which clearly had great potential, enabling the company to mount serious competition for Townsend Thoresen's operations at Cherbourg and Le Havre. This valuable link would operate from a new berth and terminal on the seaward side of the entrance to Caen's canal. At 13,505 gross tons, the *Prinses Beatrix* would be not only be the biggest ship of the fleet but also the largest ferry ever to operate out of Portsmouth.

1986

The *Prinses Beatrix* underwent a major refit in the Netherlands and was renamed *Duc de Normandie*. Brittany Ferries appointed French company AIA to redesign interior areas so that passengers would be welcomed by a taste of France as soon as they came aboard.

The main passenger lounge was named after French artist Claude Monet, who lived in the Normandy village of Giverny. The main bar boasted a calvados still and the adjoining wine bar featured a Norman cider press. The new-look ship – the company's new flagship – had her own bakery to serve French patisseries, along with a coffee shop and two restaurants.

There was more good news for Brittany Ferries passengers with the announcement that in summer the *Cornouailles* would open a new ferry link between Cherbourg and Poole – branded 'Les Routiers' after the great-value French restaurants and marketed as 'the insiders' way to holiday France – with two return crossings a day during June to September.

The *Duc de Normandie* entered service on 5th June on the 23.30 sailing to Normandy. Her extremely well-appointed accommodation introduced a refreshing sense of style and taste in ferry travel, setting new standards on the Channel and offering a real challenge to rival operators.

Well ahead of expectations, the Caen link proved overnight to be a great success. So too did the new 'Les Routiers' route, achieving great popularity and approval with travelling customers in its first season. By the end of the year Brittany Ferries had chalked up a significant new milestone, carrying more than a

million passengers for the first time.

1986 also saw Brittany Ferries inviting tenders for a new purpose-built ferry for the company's Santander route, as demand on this link continued to increase. Contracts for the new ship were signed with the French yard of Chantiers de L'Atlantique at St. Nazaire, delivery set for spring 1989. The new 24,534 gross ton vessel would be named *Bretagne* and offer cruise liner standards for 2,000 passengers, including berths for just over half that number (in two- and four-berth cabins) and space for 600 cars. Other refinements were to include 500 reclining seats in exclusive Club lounges, a 250-seat à la carte restaurant, a 430-seat self-service restaurant, a 150-seat tea lounge, two bars, a 150-seat wine bar, plus a conference room, a duty-free supermarket and an arcade of boutiques.

The *Bretagne* would be powered by four 12-cylinder Wärtsilä diesels, delivering a projected service speed of 21 knots – sufficient to cope with weather conditions encountered on this Spanish route. The task of designing the interior areas for passengers fell jointly to AIA de Nantes and the team of Rondeau and Bidault.

Another important development of 1986 was the overwhelming success of Channel Island Ferries. Sealink, which had suffered two years of heavy losses, had no option but to consider a joint operation to the islands with their rivals. But a proposed merger did not take place; after holding the monopoly for a century, the former nationalised ferry company withdrew from the Channel Islands altogether, and the new operating company British Channel Island Ferries (BCIF) was created to operate passenger-only services between Britain and the islands.

1987

In autumn Brittany Ferries announced that it planned to introduce a second ship on its Caen service during the next season (specifically, 19th May to 11th September 1988), as consort to the *Duc de Normandie*, and subsequently agreed a one-year bareboat charter of the Yugoslav-built ship *Gotland*.

1988

In June came the announcement from Brittany Ferries that it had purchased the B&I ferry *Connacht* for delivery in autumn. Built for B&I in 1978 to serve the now ceased Cork-Pembroke Dock route, the ship would undergo a £2 million refit prior to becoming the principal ship on the St. Malo route for 1989, replacing the *Prince of Brittany* and partnering the *Armorique*.

Come autumn, the company disclosed further investment in the shape of a new computer reservations system at Portsmouth. The most modern system in Britain, it would give customers a much-improved booking service. And in mid December, the former *Connacht* completed her refit in Germany for her new role, emerging as the *Duchesse Anne.*

1989

Brittany Ferries set in hand a reorganisation of the company's fleet, pending the arrival of the *Bretagne* and the introduction of the *Duchesse Anne* on the St. Malo link.

On the Caen-Portsmouth service the *Duc de Normandie* was joined by the former *Prince of Brittany*, renamed *Reine Mathilde* after William the Conqueror's queen. Following an extensive refit, she made her

Duchesse Anne *(Miles Cowsill)*

passenger debut on this route on 17th March.

The year's extra passenger sailings were complemented by the additional freight capacity provided by the newly-chartered Truckline vessel *Normandie Shipper*.

It was decided that from this year on the St. Malo route would be a seasonal service (mid-February to mid-November) rather than all year round, and the *Duchesse Anne*, the largest vessel to date to serve on the link, duly got the new season under way on 13th February, the *Armorique* joining her in May.

The plan for the *Quiberon* was to maintain the Santander, Roscoff and Cork services until delivery of the *Bretagne*, and when the new flagship entered

service the *Trégastel* would transfer to the Truckline passenger route between Cherbourg and Poole, and the *Quiberon* would become the main vessel of the premier route.

On 4th February the £55 million flagship *Bretagne* was launched at St. Nazaire. It represented the spearhead of a £70 million investment by the company. Five months later, the *Bretagne* arrived at Roscoff and after press trips on both sides of the Channel entered commercial service. The *Quiberon* was transferred as planned, enabling the *Trégastel* to move to the Truckline passenger service at Poole.

1989 proved to be a record year for Brittany Ferries, carrying some 2.1 million passengers on the six-route

network, and the company decided to expand its Truckline 'Les Routiers' service to a two-ship operation for the next season, utilising the *Corbière* and the *Trégastel*. There would be up to four passenger sailings a day during the peak season, and the combination of two passenger ships and two freight vessels would realise up to 16 sailings a day during 1990.

1990

In spring the *Quiberon* was sent for a £1 million refit to create a new restaurant, larger bar, a redesigned and expanded duty-free shopping area, new reception area and refurbished coffee shop and lounges, in preparation for the fast-expanding premier route between Roscoff and Plymouth.

In May, Brittany Ferries revealed plans to build two new vessels to replace some of the older tonnage in the fleet and to expand the Caen-Portsmouth operations. The contract for the first ferry, a new jumbo ship for the Caen service, was awarded to Kvaerner Masa Yards at Turku in Finland. A second ship for the Truckline passenger operation was also later secured with Masa at Helsinki, bringing the cost of the orders to £130 million. It would take two years to build each vessel to the new 1990 SOLAS specifications, the designs reflecting the latest international thinking on safety at sea.

The introduction of the *Bretagne*, and the ongoing investment in improving passenger accommodation and facilities across the fleet, won recognition and two national press awards from leading UK newspapers. Readers of *The Observer* voted Brittany Ferries their Favourite Ferry Company of the Year and Ivor Herbert in *The Mail On Sunday* bestowed his Car Ferry Award on the company's Portsmouth-Caen service. And another reason for Brittany Ferries to be cheerful: the Truckline passenger service between Cherbourg and Poole realised a staggering 98% increase in traffic.

1991

Barfleur, the first of the new vessels being built in Finland for the Truckline service, took to the water on 26th July prior to fitting out and completion. At 18,000 gross tons, this versatile superferry when in service would carry up to 1,200 passengers and 270 cars or, in an all-freight configuration, 118 commercial vehicles. Work progressed too on the larger Brittany Ferries vessel, the *Normandie*, due for delivery in May 1992.

Later in the year the company announced further investment – an extensive refit and upgrading of passenger accommodation for the *Duc de Normandie* for the 1992 season and beyond, and construction at Portsmouth of a new double-decker linkspan and extended berth for the new 27,000-ton flagship *Normandie*. Her huge dimensions also necessitated similar work on the French side of the Channel – a new linkspan plus a major dredging operation to enable the giant superferry to use the port of Caen in all weather conditions.

This year also recorded a further increase in carryings, the Cherbourg route growing by a very healthy 19% – success which led to the decision by

Brittany Ferries to 'jumboize' the *Barfleur*, at that time half way through construction in Finland. This size increase would create cabin accommodation for a further 200 passengers and enlarge public areas and the car and freight decks. The extra work on the vessel meant a delivery delay of some three months. In October the giant *Normandie* was floated.

1992

In March the company announced the £70 million purchase of the German ferry *Nils Holgersson* from TT-Line for use on the Spanish route, necessitating major rebuilding and overhaul of the vessel prior to her entry into service in 1993 – at which time the *Bretagne* would transfer to the St. Malo-Portsmouth route in place of the *Armorique* and the *Duchesse Anne*.

On 4th April the *Barfleur* sailed into Poole from Cherbourg for the first time and was the largest ferry ever to dock at the Dorset port – a milestone for which the Harbour Commissioners had prepared by conducting a substantial programme of dredging of the main channel. The 8-deck jumbo, with capacity for 1,304 passengers and 600 cars (or a combination of 304 cars and 66 freight vehicles), set new standards for the four-hour link. On decks 5, 6 and 7 was the passenger accommodation, comprising an impressive variety of public areas which included two restaurants, duty-free shops and boutiques, a bar and children's playroom and nursery. All 62 cabins boasted private facilities, and the reclining seating of the Club Class lounge was just as inviting.

Following her VIP days at Cherbourg and Poole, the *Barfleur* entered service, initially for freight only but

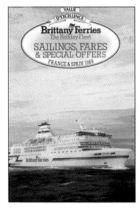

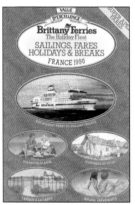

transferring to passenger operations on 15th April.

A month later Brittany Ferries' second new
superferry, the *Normandie*, left Masa Yards in Finland.
On 16th May the giant vessel sailed to Portsmouth for
her first docking as the largest ferry ever to enter the
port. Later, on the Saturday of that week, she
undertook a special VIP cruise through the Solent to
the Needles. A far cry from the early days and vessels
of Brittany Ferries, she was resplendent with 220
luxury cabins and space for 2,120 passengers and 630
cars, the latter on two decks. Her classy interior, more
akin to a cruise liner, placed the main accommodation
over four decks. The stylish areas for passengers'
pleasure and relaxation included two cinemas, duty-
free shopping mall, Le Derby bar, self-service

restaurant, the Deauville à la carte restaurant and
terrace bar, the Pays d'Auge tea shop and a most
elegant reception area to welcome passengers aboard.
And adorning the spacious air-conditioned interior
were original paintings by Normandy artists.

With an imposing 161-metre length and 26-metre
beam, here was a vessel setting eye-opening new
standards for the '90s on the English Channel, just as
the *Duc de Normandie* had done in 1986 when she
opened the Caen link.

On Monday 16th May 1992, under the command of
Captain Bertrand Apperry, the *Normandie* entered
service proper on the 08.00 sailing from Caen to
Portsmouth – and in doing so increased the capacity
on the route by some 40%.

In autumn the company announced further expansion plans for 1993, namely increased sailings between Roscoff and Plymouth and additional sailings on the Roscoff-Cork service to meet the route's growing demand. In addition, sailings to Ireland would benefit further from the mid-June opening of a new 18-hour service between St. Malo and Cork operated by the *Duchesse Anne*.

1993

Brittany Ferries took delivery of the *Nils Holgersson* from TT-Line and on 15th January the former German vessel sailed from Lübeck to Italy under her new name the *Val de Loire* for her major refit and rebuild – a

programme which would equip her for the Spanish and Irish operations. This continued and major investment by the company, not only in new tonnage but also in associated expenditure such as extensive staff training, paid handsome dividends during the year when the AA uniquely awarded Brittany Ferries a five-star rating for both the *Normandie* and the *Bretagne* – the first operator to receive the highest accolade for cross-Channel ferries.

Early in 1993 came an announcement from P&O European Ferries – Brittany Ferries' competitor on the Western Channel – that it was to open a rival UK-northern Spain service. This commenced on 28th April, the *Pride of Bilbao* leaving Portsmouth for Bilbao

Barfleur *(Miles Cowsill)*

some two months ahead of Brittany Ferries' introduction of its new ship the *Val de Loire* on the new service from Portsmouth to Santander, west of Bilbao.

1994

Despite the exceptional quality of the new tonnage the company had introduced on the Western Channel, the downturn in the British economy was to have an adverse effect on Brittany Ferries' trade. The company recorded losses for 1993/1994, due principally to the fall in the value of sterling against other European currencies at that time. Christian Michielini, Brittany Ferries' Chief Executive in France, was optimistic that the trading year of 1994/1995 would improve, no doubt encouraged by the fact that despite the losses, in 1993 the company had enjoyed an overall 5.8% increase in passenger and vehicle traffic.

At Christmas, the *Val de Loire* was chartered for a special cruise from Portsmouth to Amsterdam. The event was repeated in 1995, the destination being Rouen.

1995

Early in the year, Brittany Ferries opened talks with the Port of Bayonne in south-west France to discuss the viability of introducing a new ferry service to the French port from the UK. In the event the new service did not materialise and the company continued to concentrate on their established Santander operations.

1996

This was the year in which the Channel Tunnel

Normandie (*Miles Cowsill*)

opened, with an immediate effect on Brittany Ferries' services in the Western Channel. To remain competitive with both the tunnel and the ferry operators on the Dover Strait, the company re-structured fares. Later in the year, in the light of further losses, fares were re-structured again. Brittany Ferries and P&O European Ferries discussed the possible merger of their operations on the Western Channel, but both decided against it.

1997

Fortunately, in spite of the tunnel, fortunes on the Western Channel improved during the latter part of 1996, the pound remaining stronger against the French franc. By early March 1997, Brittany Ferries claimed that bookings were up 15% from the previous year and when summer ended were confident that bookings overall were up by some 60% compared with the 1996 season.

1998

Following a robust turnaround in both its financial and commercial fortunes, Brittany Ferries decided to restart the company's ambitious fleet renewal programme. At the AGM in March, the Chairman, Alexis Gourvennec, reported an increase in turnover, profits and passenger and vehicle carryings. He said that this revival in the company's performance was attributable to two key factors – the effectiveness of the recovery plan implemented the previous year, and the upturn in the French holiday market. During the financial year 1996-1997 the company's turnover rose by some 14.5% to show an operating profit after tax of

FF84.5 million. The company's share of the Western Channel passenger market had also seen growth during the previous 12 months – up by 6.6% to over 49%, with car traffic achieving in excess of 53%. Freight traffic too rose (by 8%), Brittany Ferries attaining 49% of the freight market on the Western Channel.

The company decided to pursue 3 key strategies: further reorganisation of the Group at the end of 1998, abandon the Truckline Ferries branding on its Poole-Cherbourg route from 1999, and bring the Poole services under the company's branding.

1999

This was the year in which the European Union put an end to the duty-free concession, thereby placing further pressure on Brittany Ferries' operating profits and on those of their English Channel rivals. But it was a setback which the company quickly resolved, adapting its onboard sales operation in a way which continues to minimise the potentially crippling effects of the EU legislation.

And in a further move to attract more business to the Western Channel, Brittany Ferries launched a revolutionary tariff policy for passengers and cars. In 2000, for the first time, no tariffs were quoted in the company's brochure, inviting customers to phone for details, as was the routine with airlines such as Easyjet. This new style of yield and fares management, utilising the speed and technology of the internet, rapidly evolved globally as the most efficient and cost-effective method to do business, and today more than 75% of bookings are made in this way.

In total in 1999, with a fleet of seven ships

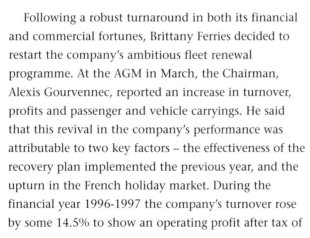

Barfleur (Kevin Mitchell)

operating over six routes, Brittany Ferries achieved a 52.2% share of the competitive Western Channel market, conveying 2,654,157 passengers, 690,891 cars and 172,291 freight units.

2000

On 27th April Brittany Ferries announced plans to build its first new tonnage since the introduction of the *Normandie*. The new £80 million vessel would serve the successful Caen route and have capacity for 175 trucks, 600 cars and 2,000 passengers – at this time the largest ship ever built for cross-Channel operations. The decision to invest in the new ship followed another year of substantially-improved financial results, Group turnover overall increasing by some 4.1% to £195 million, despite the loss of duty free.

On 11th September, after fierce competition between three European yards, Brittany Ferries revealed that the order to build this new ferry had been placed with Van der Giessen-de Noord. It was planned that on

the new ship's entry into service during 2002, she would replace the *Duc de Normandie*, the latter then transferring to the Roscoff-Plymouth service in place of the *Quiberon*, which would be disposed of. The new state-of-the-art vessel would consolidate Brittany Ferries' status as the number one operator on the Western Channel for passengers and freight.

During the same month Brittany Ferries revealed that the company was planning a joint venture with Condor Ferries, the objective being the creation of a new high-speed ferry service between Poole and Cherbourg, utilising the *Condor Vitesse* and beginning during 2001. The service would run in tandem with the conventional ferry *Barfleur*, and the Condor-owned craft would display the joint liveries of Brittany Ferries and Condor.

2001

The keel of the new Brittany Ferries vessel *Mont St. Michel* for the Caen route was laid in March, entry into service planned for May 2002. The joint fast-ferry service between Poole and Cherbourg commenced on 22nd May and ran until the end of September, proving an overwhelming success.

Coutances *(Kevin Mitchell)*

Val de Loire *(Miles Cowsill)*

During 2001 Brittany Ferries achieved further increases in traffic on the company's routes, carrying over 2.5 million passengers – a rise of some 1.4% over the previous trading year.

2002

On 15th March the *Mont St. Michel* was launched at the yard of Van der Giessen-de Noord. She had been delayed for various reasons and at the time of the launch it was anticipated that she would enter service in late July. But continued delays with construction and fitting out of the interior meant that it was not until December that Brittany Ferries finally took delivery.

In the meantime, on 5th June, the company revealed plans to build the first northern European car ferry to feature such luxurious cruise facilities as a swimming pool with lido area, and cabins with either a balcony or a terrace. The target was to introduce this innovative new ferry on the Spanish service in spring 2004. To be named *Pont-Aven* after the town in western Brittany, she would replace the *Val de Loire* on the Spanish, French and Irish routes. In summer Brittany Ferries confirmed that the new £100 million, 40,000-

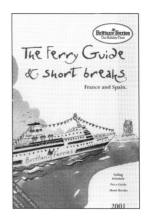

Mont St Michel *(Miles Cowsill)*

ton vessel would be built at the German shipyard of Meyer Werft, renowned for its expertise in constructing ferries and cruise ships of the highest calibre. The *Pont-Aven* would have a length of 185 metres, a 31-metre beam and the capacity to accommodate 2,200 passengers, 650 cars and 20 lorries. With a service speed of 27 knots she would be capable of reducing what was then a 24-hour crossing between Plymouth and Santander to just 18 hours.

On 20th December the *Mont St. Michel* finally entered service between Caen and Portsmouth, her arrival at last addressing the imbalance of operations on the Caen route since the delivery of the *Normandie* in 1992.

2003

On 10th April the keel of the *Pont-Aven* was laid at Meyer Werft; on 13th September she was floated at the undercover yard for further construction work.

Later in the year, the *Barfleur* completed a milestone in the history of the company, when she completed over 12,000 crossings since entering service in 1992.

2004

The *Pont-Aven*, the seventh vessel to be built for Brittany Ferries, was handed over by the German shipbuilders on 27th February, three days ahead of her scheduled delivery date. She then made her way down the English Channel to Roscoff via Caen, arriving at the Breton port on 2nd March for berthing trials. On 17th March she made her first visit to Plymouth as the *Val de Loire* was departing on her penultimate sailing to Spain. The *Pont-Aven* then made her maiden voyage

to Spain on the morning of 24th March.

For the first time, Brittany Ferries saw competition on its Portsmouth-Caen service. This came from P&O Ferries, the British company introducing a fast-ferry service. But the competition was short-lived, lasting only one season, and in any case made very little difference to Brittany Ferries as the rival service created its own market.

On 5th April the company launched the new service between Portsmouth and Cherbourg with the *Val de Loire*, the route attracting very little traffic.

In September, rivals P&O Ferries announced rationalisation plans throughout its ferry operations in the UK, including closure of its Portsmouth-Cherbourg route and the proposal to hand over its rival Le Havre service to Brittany Ferries, together with the P&O ships the *Pride of Portsmouth* and *Pride of Le Havre* which, provisionally, would be renamed *Étretat* and *Honfleur*. In the event, the company decided to withdraw from the venture due to market conditions. Subsequently, in September 2005, P&O Ferries would close its Le Havre route after operating to France on the Western Channel for more than 40 years.

2005

With the withdrawal of P&O's operations, Brittany Ferries announced that its Portsmouth-Cherbourg route for the summer would be operated by the newly-acquired fastcraft *Normandie Express*, accommodating 900 passengers and 280 cars. For four days of the week she would be employed on two round sailings a day between the two ports, and on Friday to Sunday would provide additional capacity on the Caen route. It

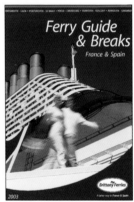

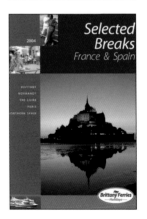

Pont L'Abbé *(Miles Cowsill)*

transpired that this new fastcraft service had a trouble-free season and achieved good loadings on both the Cherbourg and Caen routes.

During August Brittany Ferries revealed that Aker Yards in Finland was to build a new ro-ro vessel for the Cherbourg-Poole service, replacing the ageing *Coutances*. With delivery in 2007, it would have a capacity of 2,200 lane metres and 120 cabins.

In November Brittany Ferries announced the sale of the *Val de Loire* to DFDS Seaways and a medium-term

charter of the *Duke of Scandinivia* from the Danish company. She would be renamed *Pont l'Abbé* and placed on the Plymouth-Roscoff service in place of the *Bretagne*, which would return to her former St. Malo-Portsmouth route. And with the disposal of the *Val de Loire*, the company would build a new vessel for the Plymouth-Roscoff service, to be constructed at Aker Yards in Finland for 2008. This new ship would be modelled on the *Mont St. Michel* and built specifically for passenger and freight requirements between

Brittany and the West Country. Until the new ship was delivered, the *Pont l'Abbé* would continue on the Roscoff service.

During 2005, due largely to the demise of P&O Ferries' operations from Portsmouth, Brittany Ferries increased passenger and freight carryings. Passenger numbers rose by 8.8% to 2.46 million and freight increased by a dramatic 10.1% to 232,723 units. Chairman Alexis Gourvennec said that the slowdown in the market had been felt by all on the English Channel but maintained at the time that Brittany Ferries was the least affected. He also believed that the current enthusiasm for low-cost airlines could be something of a passing phase and that passenger traffic might yet return to the ferries.

2006

The chartered *Pont l'Abbe* entered Brittany Ferries service between Portsmouth and Cherbourg on 6th March prior to its transfer to the Roscoff route on 31st March. During 2006, Portsmouth Continental Ferry Port celebrated 30 years of operations, and on 6th June Brittany Ferries celebrated too – the 20th anniversary of its Caen-Portsmouth service. The two purpose-built ships the *Normandie* and the *Mont St. Michel* were dressed overall for the event.

In November Brittany Ferries revealed that its new ship for the Roscoff-Plymouth service would be named

Holidays from Ireland

Normandie Express
(Miles Cowsill)

Armorique. On the 29th of the same month, the keel of the *Cotentin* – the new freight vessel for the Cherbourg-Poole service – was laid. And at New Year, the *Pont-Aven* was employed on a special cruise between Portsmouth and Rotterdam.

2007

Alexis Gourvennec, the charismatic founder of Brittany Ferries, died in Morlaix, Brittany, on 21st February, aged 71. A man of exceptional drive and determination, he led Brittany Ferries through good times and bad to the status and position it still holds in 2012 as one of Europe's leading and most respected ferry operators. He was succeeded as President of the company by Jean Marc Roué, who hails from western Brittany.

On 12th April 2007 the new freight vessel *Cotentin* was floated out for entry into service later in the year. As the new vessel fitted out in Finland, it became clear that the *Cotentin* would be employed not only on the Cherbourg-Poole service to replace the *Coutances* but would also open a new 27-hour freight-only service between Poole and Santander. During the last week of September the *Cotentin* underwent trials from the Finnish yard prior to being handed over to Brittany Ferries at the end of October, entering commercial service on 26th November and undertaking her first trip to Spain on the 30th.

2008

Brittany Ferries celebrated the 30th anniversary of services to Spain introduced in 1978 by the *Armorique*. With an increasing number of British holidaymakers favouring sunny Spain over France, and many others opting to buy a holiday home or to retire in Spain, the company has been able to establish a consistently good year-round trade on this route.

On 10th August the new *Armorique* was launched at Helsinki in Finland. With capacity for 1,500 passengers and 500 cars, she promised ever better standards of comfort and service on the Plymouth-Roscoff route – in 1973 the company's premier route – for the 2009 season.

In autumn, the company announced an £8 million refurbishment and refit in Poland for the *Bretagne* in readiness for the 2009 season, which would mark her 20th year of service with Brittany Ferries.

During 2008 Brittany Ferries carried 2,733,655 passengers, a rise of some 2.8% on the previous year, and car traffic overall increased by some 6.4%. Freight levels dropped as the global economic crises started to bite in the last quarter of trading.

SeaFrance, the troubled short-sea operator at Calais, entered into discussions with Brittany Ferries regarding a possible take-over by the Breton company, which was declined.

2009

Prior to entering service between Roscoff and Plymouth on 10th February, the new 110 million-euro *Armorique* sailed from her builders in late January and arrived in Brest at the end of the month for crew familiarisation.

With continued growth of the UK-Spanish services, the dedicated freight vessel *Cotentin* increased her sailings from Poole to two round sailings a week.

In December Brittany Ferries announced the

Cotentin (FotoFlite)

purchase of the Greek-owned vessel *Superfast V* for additional tonnage on the Santander and Cherbourg links. With a service speed of 23 knots, the new ferry was ideal for her new role from Portsmouth, boasting two large car/freight decks and two lower holds for cars – an overall capacity of 712 cars/77 lorries.

2010

In February Brittany Ferries took delivery of the *Superfast V* from her former Greek owners, renaming her *Cap Finistère* for her new role. Considerable work was undertaken to the vessel's interior to bring her in line with rest of the fleet, the most apparent

refurbishment being the central casino area to convert it into a self-service café, Petite Marché. The new ship entered service in March.

During the week ending 22nd April 2010 – the week in which the erupting volcano in Iceland threw a huge cloud of ash into the air, grounding many aircraft – Brittany Ferries carried over 35,000 additional foot-passengers, more than 5 times the number in the corresponding week of 2009, as stranded travellers headed to Europe's key continental ports in a bid to find an alternative way home. During the flight restrictions, Brittany Ferries' reservation centre in Plymouth managed to answer 5,600 calls a day, and

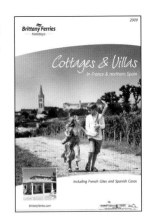

bookings for the period were up by more than 108%!

In September, P&O Ferries closed its rival service to Spain. Brittany Ferries responded with the news that for the following season it would fill the void on the Bilbao service, twice a week, with the *Cap Finistère* and offer up to 5 return sailings a week to the Iberian peninsula.

2011

In March Brittany Ferries and shipbuilder STX France revealed that they were embarking on a new joint study project to develop a new generation of environmentally-friendly passenger ferries. The new ships, powered by dual-fuel engines, will burn liquefied natural gas (LNG) in combination with a high-efficiency electric propulsion system, reducing energy consumption and CO_2 emissions by 15-20% compared with the current ferries.

On 27th March the *Cap Finistère* opened the new Bilbao service, marking Brittany Ferries' first new port destination for some 25 years. The company continued to benefit from growth on the Spanish services in spite of the global recession, although trade on the UK-France links showed a small decline due to the strong euro against sterling and the overall drop in trade in the Eurozone.

2012

In May the *Normandie* chalked up her 20th year of service on the Caen-Portsmouth link, having lost very few sailings during her long career. It is estimated that to date she has travelled 2.2 million miles – almost the equivalent of 5 times to the moon and back!

Armorique *(Miles Cowsill)*

Cap Finistère *(Miles Cowsill)*

The *Barfleur*, made available for charter in 2012 by Brittany Ferries, was duly chartered for a new venture on the Dover Strait, following the demise of SeaFrance at Calais.

In September, after 11 years, the joint operation between Brittany Ferries and Condor on the Poole-Cherbourg route was terminated. However, with continued demand for this service from Dorset passengers and freight operators, Brittany Ferries announced that the route would re-open in 2013, the *Barfleu*r making one round sailing a day.

2013

In January 2013 Brittany Ferries announced that they would open a new ferry link between Portsmouth and Le Havre using the *Normandie Express*. The vessel is due to enter commercial service on this new route on 17th May, offering one round sailing a day, four days a week.

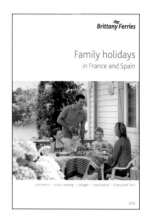

2012 FACTFILE

• Brittany Ferries now carries a million visitors a year to France, which equates to an annual total of 10 million bed nights.

• Brittany Ferries commands a higher degree of customer loyalty and repeat business than any of its competitors, 54% of customers having travelled with the company more than once.

• British visitors account for 17% of the total number of annual foreign visitors to France.

• Between 200,000 to 400,000 secondary homes in France are owned by Brits.

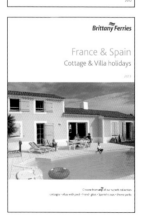

CHAPTER THREE

Leading by design

Over the company's 40-year history to date, Brittany Ferries has won admiration from a wide audience for the outstanding design quality of its ships. 'Design' is not only relevant to the naval architecture and marine engineering, but also to the overall culture of the company's operations and the way that customers and employees experience them.

Since that pioneering day in January 1973 when the business was launched, Brittany Ferries has been forever innovative. In design terms, the first purpose-built ships – the 1974 *Penn Ar Bed* and the *Cornouailles* – were somewhat functional. But both reflected the company's initial role as an exporter of Breton agricultural products, and these ships' ability to carry small numbers of passengers was a bonus. With only a limited number of cabins, the *Penn Ar Bed* could accommodate 250 passengers and the *Cornouailles* managed to squeeze in 550, about half of whom were berthed in very small cabins.

As for comfort, these initial ferries were worlds away from the very commodious and luxurious ships of today's Brittany Ferries fleet. The staircases between decks were steep and narrow and the passenger environment characterised by Formica panelling and cafeteria-style furniture. But even then, Brittany Ferries won praise for its freshly-cooked French cuisine and the cleanliness and punctuality of its ships – two benefits which made the company distinctive and put it ahead of the competition.

Another plus was the smart and distinctive all-over white livery with blue and red hull stripes. At a time when the nationalised British Railways (Sealink) operation painted its ships with dark blue hulls, and Townsend Thoresen opted for orange exteriors, the Brittany Ferries fleet presented a more modern and holiday-orientated aesthetic – a design identity which has evolved over the years to create a more elegant company logo featuring more stylish fonts, and cleverly varied to suit the design and character of particular ships.

A major turning point for Brittany Ferries was the acquisition in December 1975 of a large and well-appointed three-year-old Scandinavian ferry, the 5,732 grt *Terje Vigen*, introduced on Brittany Ferries' St. Malo route as the renamed *Armorique*. She was the first of a series of similar vessels of mainly Norwegian, Danish and Swedish origin to enter service with the company over the next decade, namely the *Prince of Brittany*, the *Goëlo*, the *Trégastel* and the *Quiberon*. All six had one thing in common: they were designed by renowned Copenhagen naval architects Knud E. Hansen A/S.

The *Terje Vigen* was up for sale in 1975 because her owner, the Norwegian Jens C. Hagen, was in financial difficulties. On Scandinavian ferry routes, competition was intense and the immediate effects of the oil crisis, coupled with spiralling increases in labour costs, meant that smaller operators such as Hagen had to sell tonnage to stay in business. Larger firms sought a solution in quickly replacing second-generation ferries with even bigger third-generation 'jumbo' ferries to achieve better economies of scale. As a result, enterprising companies such as Brittany Ferries were able to acquire recently-built 'state-of-the-art' ex-Scandinavian vessels, ideally suited for service on the western English Channel, for a song. In this respect, Brittany Ferries was fortunate to be entering the ferry business at such an opportune time; more recent years have seen several prospective new ferry business initiatives fail due to the inability to secure suitable vessels. On the other hand, it is just possible that the ever-shrewd Alexis Gourvennec, the founder of Brittany Ferries, foresaw the possibility of quickly acquiring a dominant fleet at such bargain prices.

The *Terje Vigen*, completed by the French Chantiers du Havre shipyard in May 1972 for service between Århus and Oslo, typified the design strengths of Knud E. Hansen. Utilising hoistable platform decks she could accommodate 170 cars or a mixture of cars and freight. Of her 700-passenger capacity, 410 were berthed in cabins. The public rooms were on the saloon deck

Top: **Armorique**, Cafeteria. *(Ferry Publications Library)*

Left: **Armorique**, Luxury Cabin. *(Ferry Publications Library)*

above and consisted of a restaurant and lounge bar, cafeteria and an arcade. Large expanses of panoramic windows gave good all-round views and allowed daylight to flood in – a sharp contrast to the more compartmentalised and rather gloomy spaces common to many other Channel ferries at that time. Renamed the *Armorique*, the *Terje Vigen* became a stalwart, her excellent design and comfortable accommodation contributing to Brittany Ferries' growing reputation.

The next significant ship to join the Brittany Ferries fleet was the *Prince of Fundy*, chartered in 1978 and subsequently purchased. Her layout was much like that of the *Armorique*, with 520 berths – approximately half

of her total passenger certificate – and space for 210 cars, with retractable hanging vehicle decks on either beam. Cabins were below the car deck and on both main and boat decks, although the saloon deck was nearly identical in plan to that of the *Armorique*. She operated with great success on the English Channel as the *Prince of Brittany* and, with the *Armorique*, was a key vessel in the company's growth and development.

In 1980 Brittany Ferries chartered the *Goëlo* for the St. Malo-Portsmouth route. Another former Swedish vessel but of somewhat older vintage, she began life in 1967 as the *Stena Britannica* for Stena Line's Gothenburg-Kiel service. She proved to be an excellent

Tregastel *(Ferry Publications Library)*

acquisition for Brittany Ferries' Western Channel operations, not least because her powerful 16-cylinder MAN diesels gave her a cruising of over 23 knots, ideal for maintaining peak summer schedules. Moreover, the the *Goëlo* was both beautiful externally and expensively outfitted. Stena had employed architects Rolf Carlsson and Robert Tillberg to decorate the public rooms, which were very elegant, with fine wood veneers, rich colours and mural panels. The cafeteria was above the dining saloon, aft, and the same galley served both. This was amidships on the main deck, comfortable arcades featuring on either side to connect the various facilities. Forward on the boat deck was the combined nightclub and smoking saloon, complete

with cocktail bar. And as this was a Stena ship, perhaps the most important facility (and certainly the most prominently located) was the large tax-free shop, amidships on the main deck and beside the entrance hallway.

With the funnel placed aft, much of the ship's topmost deck was open to passengers, the solarium's floor-to-ceiling windows and glass-fibre panelled roof protecting them from the elements. All in all, for passengers the *Goëlo* was a most enjoyable and attractive ship – and by far the most luxurious yet seen on the short sea routes from France to Britain. But her career with Brittany Ferries was brief, returning to her owners at the end of her two-year charter.

Top: Honfleur Restaurant
- **Duc de Normandie**.
(Miles Cowsill)

Right: L'Alambic Bar -
Duc de Normandie.
(Miles Cowsill)

In 1982 Brittany Ferries returned to Scandinavia to make yet another significant purchase – the company's biggest ferry yet. The Swedish-owned *Nils Dacke* was the third of a group of half-sisters built in Germany. The onboard restaurant occupied the full width of the front third of the ship, with a cafeteria aft. To starboard was a cocktail bar and a small pub, a duty-free shop squeezed between the two. All were accessed by a central hallway. One level below, on main deck, the majority of passenger cabins and a reception lobby were located amidships. Throughout, the ferry was panelled in synthetic wall finishes, in particular very dark wood-effect laminate panelling characteristic of many German-built ferries of that era.

Brittany Ferries renamed the *Nils Dacke* the *Quiberon* and introduced her on a new Plymouth-Santander route across the Bay of Biscay. For many years she became a popular and familiar sight in Plymouth and also sailed to Roscoff and, from there, to Cork. Given that she was designed to sail in relatively sheltered waters between southern Sweden and West Germany, she proved to be outstandingly robust on the stormy Bay of Biscay, for twenty years (up to 2002) a front-line member of the Brittany Ferries fleet.

In 1984 Brittany Ferries chartered, then purchased, the Yugoslavian ferry *Njegos*, the initial intention being to deploy her on the Portsmouth-St.Malo route. She too began life in Scandinavian waters, and although similar in appearance to the *Prince of Brittany* was a high-capacity ferry designed for busy short-distance routes. An extra upper car deck took up to 370 cars, loaded simultaneously on two levels, and she had 300 berths for night-time crossings. A very practical and useful ship, she was bought outright by Brittany Ferries for the Plymouth-Roscoff route and renamed the *Trégastel*.

The Brittany Ferries line-up of Knud E. Hansen A/S designs was completed in 1985 with the acquisition of the *Prinses Beatrix*. Built in the 1970s for the Dutch state-owned Zeeland Steamship Company (SMZ) – part of the Sealink consortium sailing in tandem with British Rail's ferries on the Hook of Holland-Harwich route – this large and unusually broad ferry could carry 320 cars or make 528 lane metres of space available for freight.

Subsequently renamed the *Duc de Normandie* by Brittany Ferries, this was to become not only the new flagship of the fleet but also the first ship on which the company consciously imposed a new and distinct design identity, Architectes Ingénieurs Associés (AIA) commissioned to create the desired new look. Headed by Bernard Bidault, the firm was not an obvious choice, best known hitherto for hospital design – though in some ways a ferry is not so dissimilar in that a lot of technology and hidden servicing must be incorporated subtly into a safe, comfortable and pleasant environment. And Bidault's practice took to ferry interior design with great enthusiasm – so much so that nowadays AIA is the leading French ship interior specialist, designing for Brittany Ferries, SeaFrance and SNCM.

The existing passenger accommodation of what was to become the *Duc de Normandie* was stripped out and a new interior created by AIA. The catering facilities were left in their original positions but renovated to reflect Gallic taste. The cafeteria, forward, was given

Above: **Duc de Normandie**. *(FotoFlite)*

the ambience of a French motorway service restaurant, with bright finishes, yellow neon and colourful artworks on the bulkheads. Aft, the restaurant was furnished in plush red to contrast with the white table linen, and a patisserie added to serve coffee and freshly-baked pastries and cakes. The finished result proved a big hit with regular travellers and the *Duc de Normandie*'s many and outstanding new facilities made her the best-appointed ship on the Western Channel. Furthermore, although AIA were restricted by the ship's original two-class layout, she effectively became the prototype for a whole new generation of ferry design. And such was her initial popularity that, very early on, Brittany Ferries also toyed with the idea of increasing her vehicle capacity by raising her superstructure and inserting an extra upper car deck.

In 1988 the company purchased the *Connacht* from B&I Line and rebuilt her along similar lines to those of the *Duc de Normandie*. She entered service as the *Duchesse Anne* but was regarded as nothing more than a stop-gap measure. Designed specifically for the stormy Irish Sea, she was very sturdy but, as with the *Duc de Normandie*, the layout of her passenger accommodation was somewhat claustrophobic, lacking large windows and curiously arranged with small rooms and hidden staircases which did nothing to aid passenger orientation.

In the meantime, in 1986, Brittany Ferries had taken the bold step of inviting tenders for the company's first brand new purpose-built ship. During the first half of this decade many so-called 'superferries' had entered service in Scandinavian waters, the largest and most impressive sailing on the Baltic to link Sweden, Finland and Germany. A visit by Brittany Ferries management to the Baltic on the Swedish-Finnish services' of Viking Line and Silja Line gave the company a whole new insight into the exciting possibilities they could offer to Channel passengers – especially in comparison with rival Townsend Thoresen.

The new ship was ordered in France with the Chantiers de l'Atlantique yard at St Nazaire. At the time, the political circumstances surrounding this decision were controversial but Chantiers de l'Atlantique certainly did construct an outstanding ship (and the only new-build Brittany Ferries vessel to be built in a French yard). Fittingly, the name *Bretagne* was announced for what would be the largest and most impressive ferry yet seen on the Western Channel. As with all subsequent new-builds for Brittany Ferries, her design was the product of a team effort involving the company's own technical staff and officers, naval architects Deltamarin and interior architects AIA. In electing to work this way, Brittany Ferries has developed an impressive reputation as a client, allowing designers to think creatively in ensuring that each ship is as memorable and user-friendly as possible for passengers and crew alike.

As the new *Bretagne* was intended to operate primarily on the relatively lengthy Plymouth-Santander route across the Bay of Biscay, it was imperative that she should have outstanding sea-keeping qualities and so a great deal of testing was carried out on prototype models to achieve the optimum hull form. Four Wärtsilä diesels were specified to give a 21-knot service speed with a margin of extra power to make up for lost time in the event of adverse weather. The vehicle deck filled the width of the hull with a centre casing. Above, the passenger accommodation was spread over three decks of the superstructure.

The *Bretagne* gave AIA's architects their first opportunity to make a bold design statement and they seized it, the ship setting new standards for ferry design in the region. Cabins filled nearly all of deck 6 and the forward part of deck 8. The purser's square featured a two-deck-high atrium and the catering facilities were on deck 7 with La Baule self-service restaurant forward and Les Abers à la carte restaurant aft. These were connected by a starboard arcade, off which were a cocktail bar and shop. On deck 8 above was a tiered show lounge aft, a café amidships to port, and reclining seat lounges to starboard. Throughout, on the bulkheads, were murals by Scottish artist and Brittany resident Alexander Goudie, and passengers appreciated them so much that Goudie was commissioned to work on subsequent Brittany Ferries ships until his death in 2004.

With extra cabins below the vehicle decks, the *Bretagne* could impressively accommodate no fewer than 2,056 passengers, 1,146 of whom were berthed. Sailing south to the sun, the *Bretagne* also featured expansive sun decks and a lido bar. In terms of aesthetics she was a highly distinctive ship, viewed from outside or onboard, and became a firm favourite with passengers, especially when transferred to the Portsmouth-St Malo route.

Shortly after the *Bretagne* entered service to considerable acclaim, Brittany Ferries began work on another two new vessels, each in its own way highly innovative. One was to be a ro-pax vessel for the company's subsidiary Truckline, to serve between Poole and Cherbourg, the other a high-capacity jumbo ferry to supplement the *Duc de Normandie* on the Caen-Portsmouth route. Both ships were ordered from the Kvaerner-Masa Yards in Finland, well established in ferry construction.

The new ship for the busy Portsmouth-Caen route was to be the *Normandie*, a name referring not only to the region but also to the legendary French transatlantic liner, and the demanding service necessitated three single crossings in each 24-hour period – two fast day sailings and one slower overnight voyage. In addition, freight demand was increasing so the new ship would need to combine the qualities of

Top: **Bretagne**, Deck 7.
(*Brittany Ferries*)

Left: **Bretagne**, Cabins.
(*Brittany Ferries*)

Top: **Val de Loire**, Le Grand Large. *(Miles Cowsill)*

Right: **Val de Loire,** Reception and information. *(Miles Cowsill)*

overnight cruiseferry, day-time ferry and ro-ro freighter. Hence it was decided to give her two freight decks, one atop the other, much like the most modern vessels on the Dover Strait, and side casings with cabins on each side of the upper vehicle deck. As with the *Bretagne*, three decks of superstructure were allocated for passenger facilities, but linked by the ship's most remarkable feature – a single continuous diagonal staircase, descending through a circular void between all three decks. Located around this, and creating an open-plan heart, would be the Information Desk, shops and seating areas. In all other respects the general arrangement was similar to that of the *Bretagne*, albeit with more reclining seat lounges and a large shop forward of the entrance hallway on the main deck.

Furthermore, with cabins to be made up for night crossings and a great deal of food and drink to be served throughout the day, careful attention was paid to the design of the *Normandie*'s 'hidden' servicing. Again, Brittany Ferries benefited from Kvaerner-Masa's accumulated ferry design proficiency and, as with modern Scandinavian ships built by the firm, a containerised system was specified to load and unload catering and hotel supplies directly to and from the galley and linen stores. This would enable the *Normandie* to be turned around very quickly at each terminal port and thus maximise her cost-effectiveness, given that on Portsmouth-Caen services ferries spend 20 of every 24 hours at sea.

The second of the new ferries to be built by Finnish yards Kvaerner-Masa was the *Barfleur* – a high-density ro-pax vessel for Brittany Ferries' Truckline operation.

Although similar in external appearance to the *Normandie*, and likewise powered by four Wärtsilä diesels, the *Barfleur* had far fewer cabin berths (228 compared with the *Normandie*'s 774), the majority of passengers being unberthed.

For the company's next fleet acquisition, Brittany Ferries returned to the second-hand market, purchasing the Baltic ferry *Nils Holgersson* from TT-Line in Germany. This 31,395 grt giant certainly had the capacity required to take over the Santander route from the *Bretagne* but was built to cross the relatively placid southern Baltic, not the Bay of Biscay. As with several German-designed ferries of her generation, the seven-deck superstructure had an entirely flat front, with deck upon deck of cabins in the forward third and the public rooms aft. Worse, the bow was bluff with a pronounced knuckle joint, meaning that she tended to 'slam' once wave heights reached more than a few metres. So in order to make the calm-weather *Nils Holgersson* fit to withstand the rigours of the Spanish service, Brittany Ferries needed to commission a major reconstruction.

Undertaken in Italy by La Spezia, it involved a complete rebuild of the bow and forward superstructure for purely practical reasons, and altering the shape of the bridge and after decks for reasons which were largely aesthetic. And with a smart new livery to break up her bulky profile and an almost entirely new interior, the formerly cumbersome *Nils Holgersson* emerged from her Italian surgery as the handsome *Val de Loire* – in many respects, almost a new ship. Brittany Ferries even purchased several large collections of ocean liner memorabilia, including

Top: The hallway on the **Normandie**. *(Ferry Publications Library)*

Left: **Normandie**, Le Deauville Restaurant. *(Ferry Publications Library)*

55

Two views of the self-service restaurant on the **Barfleur**. (*Brittany Ferries*)

builders' models of these historic ships, to display in areas frequented by passengers. As the interior designers AIA observed, a combination of historic artefacts and abstract work by critically-acclaimed Breton artists can help to create a stimulating atmosphere, particularly as Brittany Ferries believes that its ships serve a clientele who appreciate such touches and that a thoughtful and well-arranged interior can greatly enhance the already special quality of a sea voyage. After the *Val de Loire* entered service in 1993, AIA developed and refined this philosophy, the results of which were apparent in the next generation of new-builds for Brittany Ferries – the *Mont St. Michel* and the *Pont-Aven*.

The *Mont St. Michel* was intended to boost the Portsmouth-Caen route as a larger running mate for the *Normandie*, though the order was placed with a different shipyard – Van der Giessen-de Noord in the Netherlands, which since the mid-1980s had acquired significant expertise in ferry design and had devised very efficient modular construction systems. The yard's speciality was fairly standardised ro-pax tonnage and a series of almost 'standard' designs had been developed for customers such as Commodore Shipping, the Isle of Man Steam Packet Company, Irish Ferries and Blue Star Ferries. The *Mont St. Michel* emerged as an interesting mixture of a typical Van der Giessen overall form enhanced by Deltamarin and AIA-designed details, as found on previous Brittany Ferries tonnage. Indeed, although the *Mont St. Michel*'s general arrangement is practically identical to that of the *Normandie*, the two ships are not 'sisters' in any other sense.

In total the *Mont St. Michel* can accommodate 2,140

passengers (with cabin berths for 808) and 600 cars or 180 freight units. Her real distinction, however, is her superbly-appointed passenger accommodation. As with the *Normandie*, this is centred upon a grand feature staircase, rising through three decks from the purser's square. On the restaurant deck are three dining options. Located aft is what might be termed a 'gastrodôme', consisting of an à la carte restaurant to starboard and a speciality gourmet restaurant to port, and nearby is a delicatessen selling Breton speciality foods. This concept is unique to the ship and has not been tried on any other ferry before or since. The restaurant area is decorated with tableaux by Cathy Banneville and Patrick Serc, consisting of texts and images about imaginary sea voyages. The bright and airy cafeteria, with works of art by Yvonne Guégan, Aldo Paolucci and Franch Vaucelles, is forward on the same deck with an open-plan servery to port. In Le Blue Note lounge on the deck above, the rich blue colour scheme is enhanced by images of musicians by Michel Four and musical instruments in glass vitrines. Another first for Brittany Ferries is a dedicated entertainment space for older children and teenagers, with a panoramic view over the afterdecks. Spacious, elegantly decorated and benefiting from state-of-the art technical and environmental design, the *Mont St. Michel* entered service in 2002 as the biggest and most impressive ferry on the English Channel.

Brittany Ferries was already planning its next flagship – a luxurious cruiseferry for the Plymouth-Santander, Plymouth-Roscoff and Roscoff-Cork routes to displace the highly popular *Val de Loire*. The order to build her went to the experienced German yard Jos.

L. Meyer Werft of Papenburg. Its many clients included Norwegian Cruise Line, Celebrity Cruises, Aida Cruises and P&O, for whom they had built the highly-regarded liners *Oriana* and *Aurora* during the mid-1990s. As for ferries, Meyer Werft was most famous for constructing the *Silja Europa* which, on delivery in 1993, was the world's largest of her kind. Brittany Ferries' new flagship would be similarly outstanding too – particularly as everyone involved (Brittany Ferries, the shipyard, naval architects Deltamarin and interior architects AIA) had very firm ideas about how the vessel's design should be tackled. After a rapid development process, the result was a pragmatic compromise between the various factions. AIA, for example, were keen to extend their remit to the ship's external appearance to ensure that all aspects were as harmonious as possible. The final plans were for a ferry that would certainly be distinctive – 41,700 gross tons, 184 metres long and relatively low, with a highly curvaceous forward superstructure but a box-like stern.

The ship was to be named *Pont-Aven*, after the small and picturesque estuary town in southern Brittany, and the aim of the designers was to achieve an authentic 'cruise' experience – particularly important to passengers given the lengthy sailings to and from Spain. So the priority was sharply focused on creating a very relaxing and enjoyable environment, and in order to define the ambience to be achieved in each of the public areas AIA's designers Bernard Bidault, Jean-Hubert Mignot and Luc Millequant produced a series of 'mood boards', embracing colour, texture and decorative details.

Everyone boarding the *Pont-Aven* today will

Pont-Aven: Le Grand Pavois Bar. *(Brittany Ferries)*

references to Art Nouveau – a style of design found in Spain, France and Scotland in the late 19th and early 20th centuries. The restaurant's outstanding feature is its picture windows around three sides, giving spectacular views of changing seascapes in the ship's wake.

As the *Pont-Aven* was designed principally to carry sun-seeking holidaymakers, the outside deck areas were planned with great care. Large expanses of teak are the perfect base for sun-loungers, and the wrap-around promenade originally featured an enclosed viewing area overlooking the bow. Alas, stormy winter weather proved too much for the glass and for safety reasons it has since been plated with steel.

Since the *Pont-Aven* was delivered to Brittany Ferries in 2004, her passenger facilities have won widespread praise. The ship accommodates 2,400 passengers, her 650 cabins providing berths for 2,008. Her speed of 27 knots makes her one of the fastest vessels in the fleet, and she operates a very intensive schedule which in day-to-day service severely tests the design, quality and reliability of her machinery.

In 2005 Brittany Ferries chartered, and subsequently purchased, the 5-year-old InCat craft *The Lynx* (renaming it *Normandie Express*) to operate a catamaran fast-ferry service from Caen and Cherbourg to Portsmouth. High-maintenance vessels of this type require very regular servicing, but to the company's credit very few cancelled sailings have been due to technical problems. And although crew costs are very much lower than those of conventional ferries, fuel costs are far greater and it takes a highly skilled team of engineers to keep her running efficiently and to schedule.

immediately discover that the centrepiece of their grand design was the atrium. The *Pont-Aven*'s character is one of cool understatement, subtly achieved with light colours and expanses of plate glass. The main entertainment space, two decks high, is Le Grand Pavois, its colourful nautical theme continued in the adjacent lido area on the topmost passenger deck, comprising a swimming pool surrounded by teak decking, where patio doors open out to expansive sun decks. Here, large abstract ceramic panels depict Breton, Spanish, Irish and British bagpipe players. Indeed, throughout the ship, the design's general theme is the shared culture of the various countries served by the Brittany Ferries fleet.

The cafeteria and food court has a Spanish theme – bright colours and sculptures by Gérard Venturelli which depict the movement of flamenco dancers. Located aft is Le Flora à la carte restaurant, which has

Top: Les Romantiques - Restaurant (*Brittany Ferries*)

Left: The portside arcade on the **Mont St Michel**, viewed from the upper level of the entrance hallway. (*Brittany Ferries*)

Right: **Mont St Michel**, Reception and information. (*Brittany Ferries*)

Cap Finistère, Cotentin, Normandie Express. *(Brittany Ferries)*

Brittany Ferries then placed two further orders for new tonnage, replacements for older ships in the fleet, at Aker Finnyards – the former Kvaerner-Masa shipyard which built the *Normandie* and the *Barfleur*, and using the same design team. The freight vessel *Cotentin* was completed within a year and entered service in November 2007 – the month in which the keel to the other new-build, the *Armorique*, was laid in Finland.

The *Armorique* entered service in January 2009 and was built not only for the Roscoff-Plymouth service but also to be utilised out of season on other routes during refits and lay-ups of larger tonnage in the fleet. Her passenger accommodation is spread over four decks: Decks 8 and the midships part of Deck 9 are given over to cabins and, below these, Decks 6 and 7 house all public rooms, which are clad in photomurals displaying images by the Breton landscape photographer Plisson.

The entrance reception is on Deck 6. AIA's design objective here was to create a lively, animated atmosphere for passengers, achieved in two ways: making the centrepiece an impressive curving stairway which cuts through an oval-shaped void space to Deck 7 above, and surrounding the reception desk with a variety of lounge seating. To starboard is a reclining-seat lounge with panoramic views out to sea, and forward is a spacious panorama lounge, the forward and side sections of which contain reclining seats, separated from the aft section by coloured glass dividers. In the middle of the space is a café-bar. The colour scheme of green, blue and grey imitates waves breaking on the Armorique coast in various lighting conditions and seasons of the year. The precedent for the concept was the *Normandie Express*, in which the mix of reclining seat areas, lounge seating and a café-bar area proved to be highly effective.

Aft on Deck 6 are two cinemas and, further aft still, a shopping centre with two boutiques on either side of the curving promenade. Deck 7 is reached by the curving foyer staircase, emerging into a large open-plan lounge and bar area which fills the entire aft section to port. To starboard is a quiet and elegant reading room with high-backed chairs on pedestals – perfect for relaxing with a coffee and a book or maybe working on a laptop.

Forward on Deck 7 is the cafeteria, where the warmer blue, turquoise, bright green and yellow

Top: Lounge - **Armorique.** *(Miles Cowsill)*

Righ: Le Restaurant - **Armorique.** *(Miles Cowsill)*

Cap Finistère *(Miles Cowsill)*

colours were inspired by Breton beaches, shallow waters, coastal fauna and rippling seaweed. Amidships is a large U-shaped walk-in servery with free-standing buffet counters, the focal point being the serving stations around the perimeter. Curving forward from the servery are dividers with long seating banquettes, suggestive of the wide sweeps of coast found at river estuaries. And because of the *Armorique*'s midnight and mid-afternoon sailing times, it was decided that the inclusion of a dedicated waiter-service restaurant was undesirable.

Above these two main public room decks are two decks given over entirely to passenger and crew cabins. The options for passengers are standard inside and outside cabins, all with private facilities, and somewhat more spacious and luxurious Club Plus cabins.

The most recent vessel to enter service in the company's 40-year history was the German-built *Superfast V*, purchased from the Greek ferry operator Superfast. Despite their names, the twelve near-sister vessels in the Superfast series were not in fact high-speed catamarans of the likes of *Normandie Express* but 28/30 knots ferries which had been built for various services in Greece. And the clever Superfast branding and marketing was highly successful against rivals in the Adriatic and Aegean Seas.

Brittany Ferries acquired the *Superfast V* in 2009 as additional tonnage for the very successful Spanish operations and the Portsmouth-Cherbourg route. Renamed *Cap Finistère*, she is very different from the rest of the fleet, her main areas for passengers being on a single deck, with parallel arcades on either beam of the ship, each passing through open-plan restaurant/cafeteria areas to an impressive twin-level bar astern. Cabin accommodation is located over three decks and the garage/freight decks are on levels 3 and 5, with additional car deck space below the main freight deck on levels 1 and 2. As time was limited in order to make her ready for the 2010 season, Brittany Ferries undertook only minor modifications but in 2011 invested further monies on getting her up to specification for her three round sailings a week to Bilbao and Santander. As with every ship in the fleet, the *Cap Finistère* has her own distinctive identity and style and has worked well as the *Pont-Aven*'s partner on these Spanish services.

In March 2011, Brittany Ferries and shipbuilder STX France announced that they were embarking on a new joint study project to develop a new generation of environmentally-friendly passenger ferries. Powered by dual-fuel engines, the new ships will burn liquefied natural gas (LNG) in combination with a high-efficiency electric propulsion system, reducing energy consumption and CO_2 emissions by 15-20% compared with the current fleet. Pollution by nitrous and sulphurous oxides will also be eliminated.

But the never-ending quest for innovative new ideas and technology will not end there. These new ferries of the future will capitalise on lighter compound materials, high-strength glues and advanced hull design. The first of these new vessels will not only be

An artist's impression of the proposed new ferry for Brittany Ferries' Spanish service, currently under design consideration at STX Europe. *(Brittany Ferries)*

cleaner than the existing ships but larger and faster too, able to accommodate 2,400 passengers, 650 cars and 40 lorries, and cruise at up to 25 knots.

Announcing this joint venture, Brittany Ferries Chairman Jean-Marc Roué said: "Our company has a history of innovation, being based in Brittany, an area of rich maritime history, we have a profound respect for the environment and a deep understanding for the need to preserve scarce resources."

There's a great deal of work to do before these new ships can become a reality – not only in designing and developing the vessels themselves but also in creating the infrastructure necessary for their operation. In the meantime, the dominant factors in the ferry market will continue to revolve around speed, sailing times, onboard facilities and quality of service – plus, of course, the cost of oil. And as Brittany Ferries moves towards its 50th anniversary in 2023, reviewing every option will be a must.

CHAPTER FOUR

A week in the life of the *Pont-Aven*

To be hailed as a true trendsetter in all aspects of design and performance is a rare accolade in the ferry industry – yet such was the praise heaped upon the *Pont-Aven* when she entered service with Brittany Ferries in 2004.

Her striking combination of ten decks, very slick lines, high speed and luxurious interior and facilities have established her as not only a firm favourite on the Western Channel but also one of the world's leading cruiseferries.

The *Pont-Aven* was built to replace the *Val de Loire* and to offer the UK market a luxurious and speedy service to Spain. At a total build cost of 165 million euros, she represents the biggest single investment in the company's 40-year history. But the brief demanded

An artist's impression of the **Pont-Aven** prior to her entry into service. *(Ferry Publications Library)*

it: she had to be capable of making the long crossing between Plymouth and Santander in just 18 hours and cope en route with all the rigours of crossing the unpredictable Bay of Biscay. Hence speed and durability were critical factors.

Furthermore, her generous dimensions needed to extend well beyond her luxurious accommodation. The 3.35 km of garage space on the car decks was another vital necessity, taking 703 cars or a combination of up to 85 lorries and as many cars as the remaining space and configuration allowed – in line with the EU's 'Motorway of the Seas' policy, aimed at reducing the increasingly heavy road traffic in Europe by encouraging commercial transport hauliers to send their freight vehicles by ferry wherever possible. And yet another critical consideration in the *Pont-Aven*'s design and efficient operation: in most circumstances her turnaround time at each port would be less than 3 hours.

Satisfying these criteria alone was guaranteed to put her in a class of her own and set her apart from any other ferry existing at that time. Add to that Brittany Ferries' insistence on building on the company's reputation for outstanding onboard cuisine, service and passenger facilities, and it's clear that the *Pont-*

Aven was an ambitious and very bold declaration: Brittany Ferries had every intention of strengthening its status as the Western Channel's premier ferry operator.

Prior to the subsequent addition to the fleet of the *Cap Finistère* in 2010, the *Pont-Aven*'s main role on week days was serving the Spanish route, catering (in every sense) for a broad spectrum of travellers – not only holidaymakers but also more regular users of the service, particularly owners of holiday homes or other property in Spain and south-west France. At weekends, during the summer season, the *Pont-Aven* is now deployed on the important Roscoff-Cork service, a market with its own particular demands and distinctly different from that of the England-Iberian peninsula operation.

The *Pont-Aven* was named in honour of the small harbour town on the long narrow estuary of the Aven river in the heart of Cornouaille, southern Brittany. In the 18th century it was a flourishing little seaport, trading cereals with ships returning with wine and salt, and local granite was exported to England – the same granite which today adorns the striking atrium of the *Pont-Aven*. From the 1860s, art became the focus of the town's popularity as American painter Robert Wyle 'discovered' it and others followed. By the time Paul Gauguin settled here in 1886 and put Pont-Aven on the international art map, the population of 1,000 included more than 50 artists in residence – a legacy which survives today in the town's Museum of Fine Arts and variety of independent galleries, together attracting around 100,000 visitors a year.

The *Pont-Aven* was built for Brittany Ferries by

The **Pont-Aven** under construction at Meyer Werft. *(Brittany Ferries)*

leading German shipyard Meyer Werft. The yard's pedigree dates from 1795 and at the time that the *Pont-Aven* was ordered, Meyer Werft had built the *Silja Europa* – then the world's biggest car and passenger ferry. Other major MW credits have included cruise ships of the pedigree of P&O's *Aurora* and, more recently for the cruise ship market, innovative vessels for Celebrity, AIDA, Disney and Norwegian Cruise Lines.

Meyer Werft built the *Pont-Aven* over a 20-month period, delivering her to Brittany Ferries on schedule. On a very cold February day in 2004 she left the German yard and sailed up the River Ems for sea trials. She entered service at Roscoff in March, under the command of Captain Joseph Hardouin, and made an immediate and very positive contribution to Brittany Ferries' operations. Today, after 8 years' distinguished service, the *Pont-Aven* is still one of the leading cruiseferries in service in Europe.

THE INSIDE STORY

Passengers are welcomed aboard the *Pont-Aven* on Deck 6, the heart of the ship and the location of the Reception and Information Desk. But the feature which instantly inspires awe is the atrium, the full-height windows rising vertically through four decks, the uppermost being the sun deck, and topped by a glass roof to create an ambience of light and spaciousness.

Serving all passenger decks and accommodation are the atrium's main staircase and two glass lifts – design

Left: Three views of the **Pont-Aven** under construction at Meyer Werft. *(Miles Cowsill and Brian Smith)*

Top: Le Café du Festival.
(Mike Louagie/ShipPax)

Right: Les Finistères bar and swimming pool.
(Mike Louagie/ShipPax)

features inspired by the Silja Line ships *Silja Serenade* and *Silja Symphony*, themselves reminiscent of the great transatlantic ocean liners. Also adorning the atrium are large abstract paintings by Breton artist François Dilasser. Depicting circles, they bathe the walls in yellow, green and blue light.

On Deck 7 are a lounge area and a varied choice of dining options. Forward are La Belle Angèle self-service restaurant (named after Paul Gauguin's painting of Marie-Angèle Satre, reputedly the most attractive woman in Pont-Aven) and Le Café du Festival café/restaurant, which together seat up to 550 passengers – effectively two restaurants in one, designed to overcome dinner-time capacity constraints of the kind previously experienced in the *Val de Loire*'s self-service restaurant. Le Café du Festival follows the company's popular viennoiserie concept, offering a wide selection of hot and cold drinks, pastries, baguettes, pizzas, salads and the like, and La Belle Angèle restaurant is the architects' shipboard version of food courts. Separated from the dining room area by a glass wall is the oval-shaped servery and its choice of both hot and cold food.

Aft on Deck 7 is the more exclusive Le Flora à la carte restaurant and Le Fastnet piano bar. The restaurant pays homage to the work (late 19th and early 20th centuries) of Scottish designer Charles Rennie Mackintosh, and is themed on flowers and gardens, the floor-to-ceiling partitioning between the restaurant and bar resembling a garden fence and the illuminated square pillars lit from the top, reminiscent of garden lights. The high-backed chairs in the central area of the restaurant are true copies of the original

Mackintosh design, and the other seating arrangements are a tasteful combination of individual white upholstered chairs and sofas in green and burgundy tones. Adding to the restaurant's ambience are lace curtains, and calling the restaurant Flora is also significant – it was the first name of Paul Gauguin's grandmother.

Despite the restaurant's vast 350-seat dining capacity, two sittings are usually required on the busy early evening departures from Plymouth, Portsmouth or Santander. For 40 years the classic French buffet has been the hallmark of Brittany Ferries' onboard cuisine, but in recent years a variety of menus has been introduced across the fleet.

The chefs (French of course!) benefit from the training of such prestigious institutions as the Alain Ducasse School in Paris, celebrity chef Alain famed for his haute cuisine restaurants in Paris (the 3-Michelin star Plaza-Athénée), Monaco and New York. Finesse and attention to detail are a passion of Brittany Ferries too, apparent in the choice of Le Flora Restaurant tablewear, notably the textile napkins, small butter dishes and decoration dishes subtly adorned with the name *Pont-Aven*.

The decoration of La Belle Angèle restaurant and the Café du Festival, which are forward on Deck 7, employs a Spanish theme, the colours of the Spanish flag evocative of the warmth of the sunny south. Techniques used by Gaudi, a contemporary of Charles Rennie Mackintosh, feature here too, the pillars wrapped in laminated Zebrano wood and finished with rubberwork, a style repeated on the floor of the servery area. Gaudi's carved and rounded forms are also

Le Grand Pavois bar (*Brittany Ferries*)

apparent in the partitions and ceilings. The large and eye-catching abstract sculptures, depicting Spanish dancers, were created by Breton artist and teacher Gérard Venturelli and in simple terms are made of torn painted paper inserted between two resin slabs. The seating in both restaurants is a combination of yellow chairs with red, yellow and black sofas, and the Café du Festival offers diners a further pleasure – spectacular views forward through large picture windows. And lorry drivers are well catered for too, their 46-seat private dining facilities located adjacent to the restaurant and cafe area.

For passengers who enjoy the pleasures and savings of onboard shopping, Deck 8 is a big attraction – the main retail area, designed as an all-in-one shop segmented into smaller individual boutiques, each with its own checkout. This 'mall' concept is unique within the Brittany Ferries fleet, all other ships having separate retail boutiques.

And for those in search of entertainment or quiet relaxation, Le Grand Pavois bar is the place to find it. Serving as the main show lounge, this comfortable area is distinctive for its high glass roof and tiered upper-level mezzanine bar on Deck 9, also giving access to the very popular all-weather Les Finistères swimming pool and its poolside bar. On warm and sunny days the doors on both sides of the enclosed pool are opened.

As for cabin accommodation, the *Pont-Aven* offers passengers a choice of 8 categories, from standard 2-berth inside cabin to Commodore class – 4-berth suites with balcony. Of the 208 outside cabins, 12 are 2-berth and the remainder are 4-berth. In addition to

Top: Le Flora restaurant.
(Mike Louagie/ShipPax)

Right: Commodore Class
Cabin. *(Mike Louagie
/ShipPax)*

Commodore, the luxury cabin options include 56 Club class (Deck 5) and 16 de luxe staterooms (aft, Deck 8). Deck 8 also has 18 Commodore class suites. Club class are somewhat larger than standard 4-berth cabins and, in common with de luxe and Commodore, provide flat-screen TV and facilities for tea and coffee. And to enhance the maritime character, cabins are richly furnished with laminated wood and custom-made carpets, in keeping with all public areas.

Commodore class cabins on Deck 8 are complemented by a Welcome Desk and lounge, the area and corridors resplendent with watercolour paintings by Yvon Le Corre showing the *Pont-Aven* at various stages of her construction. In a similar vein, the Commodore balcony cabins – the first on any ferry serving the UK – are named after painters associated with the town of Pont-Aven, Gauguin and Emile Bernard being cabins each distinctive for its large private terrace.

Passengers opting for the luxury of Commodore class benefit from very spacious accommodation. There are two beds, a convertible sofa-bed and a fourth bed which folds flush into the ceiling. Colours of carpets and chairs are typical of the work of Gauguin and his followers, and wall coverings are a combination of laminated sycamore, deep Zebrano wood and textiles. Room service is provided too, breakfast in particular welcomed by occupants.

The deluxe cabins in this part of the ship are named after French, Spanish and British islands, and as in Commodore class an explanation of the cabin's name (as in artist or island) is given in three languages. The keys of Commodore cabins and de luxe suites give access to the Commodore lounge at the rear of Deck 8. This has all the trappings reminiscent of a liner-style club atmosphere but brought up to date – leather-upholstered chairs, six sofas, wooden venetian blinds and complimentary newspapers and drinks, the latter served at designated times during the day.

Cabins for members of the crew are in the aft part of Deck 5 and the front part of Deck 9, each having an individual cabin. They also have their own dining area and between shifts can relax in dedicated lounges – essential facilities, given that on summer sailings they often need to satisfy the demands of 2,000 or more passengers.

As flagship of the fleet, the *Pont-Aven* maintains a strict and taxing weekly schedule which begins on Friday at Roscoff with a 252-nautical mile sailing to Cork, returning to Roscoff on Saturday to sail to Plymouth and position herself in readiness for her two services to Spain – the first the 424-nautical mile crossing to Santander, with a return to Portsmouth. Just three hours later she's back at sea and heading for Spain again (516 nautical miles) and will return to Plymouth. The final leg of the week's journeys is to Roscoff on Friday morning. In winter the ship covers on the Portsmouth-St Malo route, as well as operating to Spain.

THE MAN AT THE HELM

Captain Gilles Quéré is the man responsible for not only maintaining this exacting schedule but also for the smooth running and management of the ship in all of its many facets. Gilles joined Brittany Ferries in 1984 as Mate of the *Cornouailles* on a two-day contract to move her from St. Malo to Le Havre.

From the *Cornouailles* Gilles joined Brittany Ferries' *Breizh-Izel*, affectionately known in the company as the 'cauliflower ship', on the Roscoff-Plymouth route, and later in the season moved to the *Bénodet* and the *Prince of Brittany* as Chief Officer. In the earlier days of Brittany Ferries work for officers was seasonal and in winter was confined to the coastal ships around France. But in 1986, with the opening of the company's Caen service, full-time working became the norm to man the fleet of six ships operating on the Channel and to Spain. As Chief Officer, Gilles went to Rotterdam to collect the *Duc de Normandie* after her conversion for the Caen-Portsmouth service – a significant moment in the history and development of Brittany Ferries, as this vessel was set to make the greatest impact on the company's fortunes: the opening and subsequent success of the new Caen-Portsmouth route resulted in the fleet's rapid growth.

Gilles' first appointment as Captain was on the *Reine Mathilde* alongside Captain Bertrand Apperry in 1989. As is common practice for younger captains, he was switched between various ships and routes, particularly out of season, gaining experience on the Santander, St Malo and Ouistreham services and serving for awhile in Jersey and Guersney with Channel Island Ferries.

When the Finnish-built *Normandie* entered service in 1992, Gilles was transferred to her during her first season, and later in the decade enjoyed a longer spell on the St. Malo-Portsmouth route aboard the *Bretagne*.

In 2000 Gilles was appointed Fleet Director of Brittany Ferries – a desk job in Roscoff very different

Top: Captain Gilles Quéré and his bridge team - Christophe Bergeroux (chief officer), Louis Claeyssens (mate) and Michel Le Mogne (seaman). *(Miles Cowsill)*

Left: Captain Gilles Quéré in discussion with with his Chief Engineer Robert Le Noan. *(Miles Cowsill)*

Right/à droite: Marlene Diez updates the Captain on special passenger arrangements for Santander. *(Miles Cowsill)*

from being at sea and experiencing those magical landscapes and sunsets. But in July 2007 he returned to sea as Captain of the *Pont-Aven* – a privilege he cherishes every single day. Indeed, no two days on the *Pont-Aven* are the same. Gilles commences duty at around 06.30, the bridge officers updating him of any overnight developments and the weather forecast for the coming 24 hours. At this time of day, before the majority of passengers are up and about, he takes the opportunity to walk around the ship.

"After calling at the information desk to speak to the night watchman and discuss any problems, and before going to the officers' mess, I can't resist passing by the galley or patisserie – the aroma of hot croissants is absolutely delicious!"

Breakfast with his fellow officers is followed by a meeting with the Chief Engineer Robert Le Noan and Chief Purser Jean-François Raoul to go through the ship's schedules for the day and anticipate any operational problems .

"Once we are all satisfied that our respective departments can meet the challenges of the day, it's time to read my inevitable deluge of emails and reply to them," says Gilles. "In my early days at sea there were no satellite communications, emails or mobile phones. The commercial and operational pressures are different and we are now in regular touch with the services ashore - and they're always very demanding of a quick response.

Having dealt with the essential clerical work, Gilles invests a couple of hours talking to all the crew at their posts, from the shops to the engine room and from the garage to the bars, and satisfying himself that

Top: In Le Flora restaurant prior to lunch with Philippe Gueguen and Magali Bellec/Au restaurant Le Flora en compagnie de Philippe Gueguen et Magali Bellec

Left: In the galley with head chef Patrick Bechennec. *(Miles Cowsill)*

Top: Yveline Martin and Claudie Mahé at Le Café du Festival. *(Miles Cowsill)*

Right: Pierre Marc Vidcoq maintaining the outside decks/. *(Miles Cowsill)*

everything is functioning as it should be and that passengers are receiving the expected standards of first-class service. After-lunch management meetings once or twice a week also provide the perfect opportunity to discuss the everyday running of the *Pont-Aven*.

"We have to look forward all the time – anticipating problems before they arise is so important. Then there's the ship's annual refit, which has to be meticulously planned well in advance."

Each ship in the fleet is run as an individual entity – effectively, a company in its own right, the onboard management team duty-bound to ensure that it's operating as economically and cost-effectively as possible.

"Our meetings also cover safety training and any further new legislation which has come on stream. Onboard lifeboat drill is undertaken once a week, at Cork or Roscoff."

A lighter side of the Captain's day-to-day duties at sea is talking to passengers and making sure they are enjoying the unique Brittany Ferries experience. But in inclement weather he needs to spend more time on the Bridge. "Bad weather can be stressful and tiring for the officers, but experience teaches you to cope with it."

Another demanding but very satisfying highlight of any crossing for the man at the helm is manoeuvring safely in and out of harbour on departure and arrival respectively. And having completed a week's duty onboard, Gilles is only a short drive from Roscoff to his home at St-Pol-de-Léon, where he can see the ships arriving and departing from the port. "A week at sea goes so quickly," he reflects. "And the years are just steaming by!"

Bretagne *(Miles Cowsill)*

CHAPTER FIVE

A purser's life: 24 hours aboard the *Bretagne*

Guaranteed pride of place in the fleet history of Brittany Ferries is the *Bretagne* – the first purpose-built ship to be commissioned by the company, and originally intended for the Plymouth-Santander service as a replacement for the *Quiberon*. In 2012, 23 years on, she remains one of the fleet's most popular vessels, and since transferring to the St. Malo-Portsmouth service in 1994 has won many fans amongst the route's regular travellers.

Today the *Bretagne* sails between the two ports on a 24-hour rotation, the officers and crews working for a week onboard followed by a week off.

"I joined Brittany Ferries in 1987 and my first vessel was the *Armorique*," recalls Mario Stevelinck, the ship's Purser. "From there I moved on to the Spanish service, and launched the new *Armorique* 3 years ago. I've been on the *Bretagne* for the last year and the ship has a wonderful atmosphere and is a pleasure to be aboard. The accommodation is spacious and well designed and the crew work very well together."

The St. Malo-Portsmouth service carries around 400,000 passengers a year, the busiest period being from the beginning of May to the end of October.

"The clientele varies," says Mario. "Some UK passengers are heading to Brittany for their annual holiday and others own houses or holiday homes in France and they cross the Channel regularly. Part of this route's great tradition is to enjoy dinner or lunch onboard – especially as the emphasis is on 'enjoy'. The *Bretagne* offers passengers the very best cuisine on the Channel. As I'm Purser, some people will say that I'm biased – but the praise comes not from me but our customers. Every day they make a point of telling us how much they enjoy everything we serve to them."

Mario's day aboard ship starts at around 05.45. "Normally, when we're sailing overnight from Portsmouth, I can see Jersey in the distance from my cabin window. I say 'normally' because no two days are the same – that's what makes the job so interesting. And my early start means that the ship is quiet and peaceful – most passengers are still asleep. My first task is to get an update on anything that's happened overnight – although if I haven't been called I can be sure that any queries or problems have been resolved by the night auditor."

During the high season Mario manages a team of more than a hundred crew, looking after cabins, restaurants, kitchens, bars, shops, stores and entertainment.

"It's important to me that I greet them first thing in the morning, starting at the stores and passing through the kitchens, restaurant, self-service, tea

Top: Mario Stevelinck at the entrance to Les Abers Restaurant. *(Miles Cowsill)*

Right: Les Abers Restaurant. *(Brittany Ferries)*

lounge, reception accounts office, cabins and hotel department – and not forgetting my four 'right-hand' men and women: the Head Chef, Restaurant Manager, Hotel Manager and Stores Manager.

"In the meantime, all food outlets have opened and some passengers are making their way to breakfast as the ship steadily approaches St. Malo, about an hour from docking. In the office I'll read and send messages and organise the day. Checking my agenda I'll see if any visitors are expected during the call at St. Malo, or any whether there are any special requirements for those who might be travelling with us. By this time we're only half an hour from arrival – the shops are open and the ship is a hive of activity. This gives me another opportunity to walk around, greet the staff and say hello to passengers who are shopping."

When the ship docks, Mario goes to the reception area to help direct passengers and wave them goodbye. "Our call in port is only a short one – 2 hours – so there's no time to lose. As soon as the gangway's in place, an army of cleaners rushes aboard to start preparing and cleaning cabins and public areas. Then there are deliveries of clean linen and store provisions to attend to, along with welcoming any visitors. In this period I also call in on the Captain to talk about various issues and events, and pay a quick visit to the bridge to discuss the day's weather conditions."

Boarding for the return crossing starts about an hour before departure. "Then it's time to welcome and greet the new passengers," says Mario. "After this, and depending on the day of the week, there are meetings about matters such as financial results, targets, health and safety, security, and forecasting and preparing the figures for staffing requirements for the month ahead."

Lunch for Mario is in the officers' mess, then it's a walk around all the catering outlets and shops to make sure everything's going smoothly, and calling in on the hostess at reception for any specific requests or queries."

Mario's hectic coming-and-going working life at sea means that during the afternoon he is only able to take a short rest, before he is back undertaking further office duties. "I have to find time to catch up with e-mails, organising and checking on standards in various departments, moving longer-term projects forward and dealing with anything else that crops up."

It's also Mario's day-to-day responsibility to look at the previous day's takings and check the onboard spend per head. "Meeting these targets is very important. Each vessel in the fleet is run as an independent operation and the weekly budgets have to be adhered to."

When the weather's fine and sunny, Mario spends time on the outside decks chatting to passengers.

"As the ship approaches Portsmouth on the return leg it's almost 18.00 hours and time for me to prepare again for saying goodbye to the passengers. When they've disembarked I make sure everything's in place for the crossing back to St. Malo – that the restaurant and hotel managers are aware of any special requests and the restaurant bookings have been dealt with. This just about gives me time for dinner in the mess.

"Shortly after 19.00 hours, passengers start boarding again and I welcome looking after any who require special attention. At 20.15 we set sail and I make my presence known in the onboard shops, restaurants,

Bretagne (Brittany Ferries)

bars and so on, talking to passengers and making sure they're happy and that everything's running smoothly.

"When I'm satisfied that the second seating in the main restaurant is working well and that all passengers have been seated and the Restaurant Manager is happy, I go back to my office to check the day's final emails from HQ in Roscoff. With the paperwork taken care of, I enjoy a final stroll around the ship – on a clear night very rewarding, as I can make out the distinctive lighthouses of the Cherbourg peninsula, Alderney and the Casquets. It's the perfect prelude to a well-earned sleep!"

CHAPTER SIX

A taste of French hospitality

If it hadn't been for artichokes, Brittany Ferries may never have gone into business at all. When those Breton farmers decided in the early '70s to target their neighbours across the Channel as likely customers, they could never have foreseen how a company founded on vegetable transport would have such a major impact on tourism.

The story of that first New Year's Day freight service is the stuff of which corporate legends are made. Packed with lorries carrying artichokes and cauliflowers, the *Kerisnel* set sail from Roscoff to Plymouth to deliver its fragile cargo to a country newly admitted to the Common Market.

Forty years on, the ships are still packed with fresh produce, but nowadays these quality raw materials are just as likely to be found in the restaurant kitchens as below deck. With the launch in 1978 of ferry-inclusive holidays, Brittany Ferries quickly became as well known for its passenger service as for its freight traffic, and passengers – and crew – needed to be fed.

Today's passengers have an appetising choice ahead of them and for many, onboard dining is one of the highlights of the travel experience, if not the whole holiday. Self-service café, piano bar or gastronomic restaurant are the tempting options. Brittany Ferries' onboard catering operation has always been based in Roscoff, but four decades on it takes a far more sophisticated operation to consistently satisfy diners' high expectations and taste buds.

When Jacques Le Rouzo was appointed Brittany Ferries' first Director of Hotel Services in 1977, it was company policy to employ redundant sailors from the French Merchant Navy. So rather than the qualified chefs and serving staff he needed, Jacques found himself faced with a hospitality team who first and foremost were seamen. And although the traditional French fare served onboard the company's first new-build ship the *Penn-Ar-Bed* was all freshly prepared, little thought was given to its presentation and service.

Christian Michielini, the managing director who hired Le Rouzo, remembers sending his new recruit on an initiation tour of three ships before confirming his appointment. An elegant and charismatic man, Le Rouzo knew the hospitality industry inside out but Michielini felt sure that he wouldn't be prepared for the system he'd discover onboard ship.

Sure enough, Le Rouzo declared on his return that he'd never seen anything like it – shirt-sleeved staff decorated with tattoos and showing scant regard for health and safety. His reaction confirmed to Michielini that he was the right man for the job – someone who would make sweeping and long-lasting changes.

The twin aims of the new catering regime were to introduce training and professionalism to the catering staff, and to separate the accounts of the catering department from that of the fleet as a whole. Only then would Brittany Ferries' hospitality department achieve the exacting professional standards required. But it didn't happen overnight.

The new philosophy received enthusiastic support from the Brittany Ferries management team in England, and the Wagon restaurant onboard the *Cornouailles* was the first to benefit from the new ideas. It wasn't unknown for the team in England to bring British workmen onboard whilst a ferry was in port and lay smart new carpets or carry out what they saw as essential cosmetic repairs. Restaurant staff were still largely inexperienced in hospitality, but now at least they were well turned out and had the benefit of rigorous training to meet the ever-more-demanding expectations of the British travelling public.

The team embraced new catering technology, introducing innovative ideas and labour-saving gadgets such as microwave ovens and deep-fat fryers. As new equipment was introduced into the kitchen, greater emphasis was put on health and hygiene. In the early days, customers could freely slice meat from a help-yourself counter – unthinkable in 2012! – but for the last twenty years and more Brittany Ferries has employed the services of an expert medical advisor in order to keep at least one step ahead of safety regulations.

Soon a thoroughly professional hospitality department began to take shape, boosted by the opening in 1978 of the first routes to Spain. Passengers spending almost twenty-four hours onboard ship clearly needed a bigger choice of eating and drinking options in addition to stylish and well-designed and appointed areas in which to relax in cruise-style comfort.

The first ship in the fleet to satisfy these demands was the *Armorique*, resplendent with plush carpet and comfortable chairs, encouraging passengers to do nothing but enjoy the journey. Other ships were slower to embrace the new cruise-style concept, and on most routes the menu was still basic French cuisine which owed more to tradition than to innovation. 1970s' design technology also meant that in rough weather cooking at sea could be quite a challenge, the roll of the ship making it difficult for kitchen staff to hold on to appliances and ingredients.

But to the delight of passengers, standards both behind the scenes and at front of house steadily improved. Prior to this happier state of affairs, an outraged British customer had written to Christian Michielini complaining of a catalogue of disasters and vowing to never sail again with Brittany Ferries. But a few years later, after reluctantly making another crossing with the company, the same person felt compelled to write again and express the pleasure of a much more satisfying and positive experience.

The first truly professional chefs arrived onboard in the 1980s, bringing with them a wealth of experience from restaurants and hotels across France and beyond. Catering Manager Yvon Rivoallan joined the company in 1984 and recalls that the cuisine on offer then was sadly lacking in creativity. So he immediately set about convincing his team that it was possible to offer

innovative, interesting dishes without spending more money.

"It was a mini revolution which began in the kitchens. For the first time, the Chef de Cuisine wasn't only catering for the crew but for passengers as well, and I worked onboard ship in that position during the high and shoulder seasons between 1984 and 1989, alternating with Alain Le Petit. His vast experience in catering aboard liners such as the *France* complemented my own experience of working in the kitchens of hotels such as Relais et Château. Between us we were able to develop new services for Brittany Ferries'

passengers, and through these years at sea I acquired a real insight into the conditions and challenges of cooking onboard ship, and the professionalism demanded to achieve and exceed the high standards expected.'"

During winter months spent on land, the buffet system was one of the first elements to come under review. Restaurant menus at the time specified 'Help yourself' but plates were woefully small which didn't please hungry customers. Presentation was equally low-key, hors d'oeuvres and desserts arranged on stainless steel platters intended for baking and roasting.

But as the department lacked suitable serving dishes, new tableware was called for. The company's first new-build ship, the *Bretagne*, launched in 1989, was the first to offer full-scale, mouthwatering buffets which appealed in both content and presentation.

In tandem with the buffet revolution came the development of the Brittany Ferries catering bible, launched in 1985 to replace a basic reference manual which contained photographs of the limited dishes on offer. The invaluable new aid covered every aspect of onboard hospitality, from the ingredients in each recipe and how to prepare them to the correct way to lay a table and serve wine. Still in use today, the manual is annually updated and refined in consultation with key staff from each department and taking into account the changing tastes of core customers from Britain, France and Spain. It's a vital tool, bringing together every element of Brittany Ferries' onboard hospitality and ensuring that every ship in the fleet achieves the same consistently high standards in food, drink and service.

In the second half of the 1980s, the company saw a huge diversification in its clientele as more and more families travelled to France for their holidays, many leaving Britain for the first time. The *Bretagne* was the first ship designed and equipped to cater for such a wide spectrum of tastes and budgets, a concept developed further during the 1990s.

Before this, in 1987, the unmistakeable aroma of delicious baking was wafting through the air in Roscoff. The man responsible was Brittany Ferries' master pâtissier Serge Hinault, given the job of building a department of trained pastry chefs capable of consistently creating desserts, cakes and breakfast pastries of exquisite taste and quality for the entire fleet. His success can be gauged by the fact that today, on longer ferry crossings, the dessert buffet is not only a temptation in itself but a cruise highlight for many passengers. In peak season, a team of 8 highly-skilled pâtissiers works 7 days a week, each pâttisier creating

65 large pâtisseries every day – each of which is mixed, shaped and lovingly assembled by hand.

As is true of all catering staff, Serge's team members are sent on rotation for top-level training courses to study under such legendary French chefs as Paul Bocuse and Alain Ducasse – the perfect recipe for learning fresh skills and new ideas which can be turned into delicious dishes for passengers. Such dedication and attention to detail reaps its own rewards *and* awards, Brittany Ferries regularly winning the latter from discerning readers of British newspapers such as the *Daily Telegraph* and the *Observer*, and by the members of travel organisations such as the Automobile Association.

And success, of course, breeds success. Brittany Ferries' enduring reputation for culinary excellence enables the company to recruit some of the very best chefs and restaurant and bar staff in the business, the rewards for whom include first-class training and opportunities, a genuine career path and working conditions befitting the fleet of modern and superbly designed and equipped cruiseferries.

Variety is another attraction. Depending on the season, there can be from six to ten people working in a ship's kitchen under the Chef de Cuisine, each with a specific role but capable of turning a professional hand to anything – a system which promotes excellent teamwork amongst a diverse group who must not only live and work in close proximity for seven days at a time but also consistently create dishes worthy of any esteemed mainland restaurant. As in the early days of Brittany Ferries, the cuisine is unmistakably French but the simple salads of the buffet table have given way to

piles of succulent seafood and elaborate savouries, and passengers are just as likely to dine on rack of pork cooked in hay or spicy duck with beans and Serrano ham as on traditional boeuf bourguignon.

And just to make sure that the passenger experience is as good as it can possibly be, hospitality staff swap places from time to time – a practice which originated in 1978 with the passenger and freight ship the *Pont l'Abbé*, waiters and kitchen staff taking it in turns to eat together as 'customers' and seeing first hand the quality of food and service, and exchanging ideas on how to improve both.

Brittany Ferries' catering department still works to those same principles established in 1977 when the first Director of Hotel Services was appointed. Across the years the main concern has always been to follow the development of the market and current trends, and to offer people the best possible product in terms of quality and price. Every year the department adjusts its menus and services according to feedback from customers and key staff onboard, and analyses which products are the most popular. Likewise, investment in equipment, tableware and ways of communicating with passengers is a continuous process.

Since those early days, many things have contributed to the improvements in onboard hospitality so apparent today – not only the addition to the fleet of new-build and refurbished ships but also factors such as training with external experts and the rigorous introduction of health and food hygiene regulations.

The catering department is proud to have achieved the goals set for the restaurant operation all those

years ago, but the team are never complacent and are always striving to improve. It's a constant challenge to stay ahead of what customers expect, to improve turnover, and to stay faithful to the budgets and objectives set by management.

In 40 years of providing onboard hospitality, many lessons have been learned – and none more important than the fact that as passenger tastes and expectations change as inevitably as day follows night, anticipating and catering for them is a never-ending circle. The pleasing news for Brittany Ferries is that full tables and clean plates are a satisfying indication of a job well done.

CHAPTER SEVEN

The art of ferry travel

In the same way that the creation of Brittany Ferries as a maritime business has developed strong economic and commercial ties between Brittany and the countries and regions served by the company's ships, art has the power to express and forge cultural links and to open hearts and minds to the true pleasures of travel and discovery.

Furthermore, the idea of taking works of art to sea to enhance the travel experience was established by famous ocean liners such as the *France* and Cunard's *Queen Mary* and *Queen Elizabeth* in the golden age of transatlantic voyages. And given the enduring global fame of Normandy's Impressionist painters and Brittany's 19th-century art movement centred around the small estuary town of Pont-Aven, it was a tradition which Brittany Ferries was naturally keen to perpetuate.

The first Brittany Ferries ship to apply the concept was the *Bretagne*, renowned Scottish-born artist Alexander Goudie contributing paintings, frescoes, bas-reliefs and even the menu design, all of which were complementary to the colours and themes chosen by the ship's interior design team.

After the *Bretagne* came the *Normandie*, the *Barfleur*

and the *Val de Loire*, each with its own distinct personality and character serving to leave a lasting memory in the minds of passengers. And in the process of selecting appropriate names for the current fleet's new-build ships, Brittany Ferries had decided at an early stage that *Pont-Aven* was a must.

The small Breton town and port of Pont-Aven (according to an old saying, "a town of renown, fourteen mills and fifteen houses") became a magnet for post-Impressionist painters. The first to establish a base here were American, led by the pioneer Robert Wylie, but the artist most often credited for putting Pont-Aven well and truly on the art map was Gauguin (1848-1903), his revolutionary artistic movement becoming known as the School of Pont-Aven. Today's visitors to the Pont-Aven Museum can learn and see the full and fascinating story.

With the addition to the fleet of the new ship *Pont-Aven* came the perfect opportunity to explore, in artistic terms, not only the differences between the Brittany of old, rich in legend and myth, and the more dynamic and enterprising Brittany of the 21st century, but also the idea that the town of Pont-Aven symbolises a coming together of land and sea.

Top left: **Bretagne**.
(Brittany Ferries)

Middle left: **Bretagne**.
(Brittany Ferries)

Far left: **Duc de
Normandie**. Brittany
Ferries)

Bottom left: **Duc de
Normandie**. (Brittany
Ferries)

Right: **Duc de
Normandie**. (Brittany
Ferries).

Thus the ship's interior decoration is the combined work of architects, contemporary painters, sculptors and photographers collaborating as a team and focusing on Brittany's lifestyle, festivities, music and dance. More than 200 original works of art are displayed onboard, from oil paintings, drawings, pastels, sketches, photographs and illustrations to ceramics, glass, stained glass, calligraphy, sculpture, ships in bottles and small-scale models of sailing boats.

Similarly, the arrival of the new ship *Mont St Michel* in 2002 presented its own theme – the celebration of Normandy as a birthplace of the arts, and home to not only the Impressionists and some of the most famous 19th-century novelists but also, in much more recent years, to film makers attracted by the choice of stunning locations such as Deauville, Étretat and Mont St Michel itself.

Aboard Brittany Ferries' *Barfleur* (as with all ships in the fleet), the art works adorn not only the public areas but those used by the crew. For example, in the self-service restaurant are paintings by Jean-Philippe Aubanel, in the crew and hostess messes are pastels by Pierre Caro, and in the officers' mess are paintings by Bernard Delaunay and Aymery Rolland. Other contributors whose work is presented on the *Barfleur* include photographers Philippe Dufour, Antoine de Givenchy and Denis Cadiou, and artists Catherine Viollet and Yan Zoritchak, the latter's creations in glass.

"As it was expressed so admirably by Christian Michielini, the company's longest-serving Managing Director, art brings us something extra – a chance to dream and a means of escape," says Erwann Rougé,

Barfleur

Val de Loire

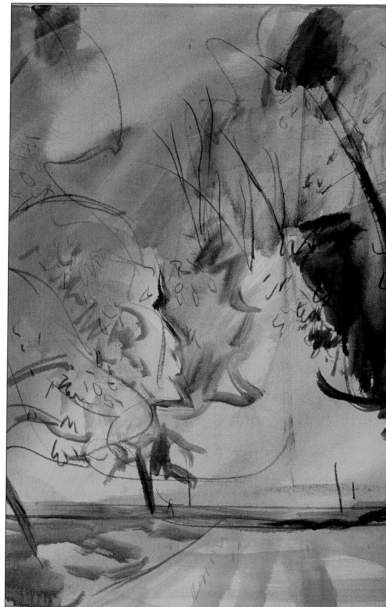

Top left: Normandie.
(*Brittany Ferries*)

Middle left: Normandie.
(*Brittany Ferries*)

Bottom left: Mont St
Michel. (*Brittany Ferries*)

Right: Barfleur. (*Brittany
Ferries*)

former Brittany Ferries' Artistic Consultant. "When you travel on our ships you have that same opportunity to discover that art is a voyage in itself. And rather than settling for hanging a few pictures, we took the bold step of commissioning original works directly from the artists themselves. These artists then work closely with the interior design specialists when a new vessel is being prepared to join the fleet.

"The aim is for each ship to give passengers more than the comforts and service they expect – to surprise them, offer them an experience that will help leave a lasting memory. Art has the power to do this. On the other hand, art is very much a creative gamble. Brittany Ferries in no way claims to be a barometer of artistic tastes or trends – and, of course, passengers will always make up their own minds. But at least we're providing that opportunity."

Pont-Aven

Top left: **Val de Loire**.
(Brittany Ferries)

Bottom left: **Mont St Michel**. *(Brittany Ferries)*

Middle: **Mont St Michel**.
(Brittany Ferries)

Far right top: **Pont-Aven**.
(Brittany Ferries)

Far right botton:
Armorique. *(Miles Cowsill)*

Y.GUÉGAN

CHAPTER EIGHT

Inimitable Brittany Ferries

From the very beginning, the conception and birth of Brittany Ferries was a unique event, and certainly within the history of the European ferry industry. And 40 years on, the company continues to innovate and develop in its own very distinctive and inimitable way.

The driving force behind the company's creation was the ambition to put Brittany on the map and open the region up to the rest of Europe and beyond – a goal which to a large extent has been achieved. In terms of social and economic stability and growth, Brittany Ferries is a significant contributor, in 2011 generating income of 198 million euros (£158.5 million) for Brittany, 82 million euros (£65.5 million) for Normandy, 92 million euros (£73.7 million) for the Pays de Loire and achieving 9.3 million bed nights for the French tourist industry as a whole, Brittany's and Normandy's share being 3.2 million and 1.3 million respectively.

As for job creation in France and England, Brittany Ferries employs between 2,239 people (low season) and 2,935 (high season), and indirectly supports a further 4,500 jobs.

The company's current fleet of 9 modern ships (more than 5,300 sailings in 2012) connects France to England and Ireland, and England to northern Spain, in the process presenting freight businesses with a practical and cost-effective 'Motorways of the Sea' alternative to the growing problems inherent in international road haulage.

More than 2.5 million customers a year (85% of whom are British) travel with Brittany Ferries and experience the joys of refined French cuisine, fine wines, attentive service, a relaxing and sophisticated ambience, panoramic sea views, onboard shopping and, on some ships, personal indulgences such as beauty and relaxation treatments.

ALL-IN-ONE HOLIDAYS

There have been many milestones in Brittany Ferries' 40-year adventure, one of the most significant, successful and enduring being the natural and logical progression from ferry operator alone to tour operator too.

Self-drive package holidays to France became a reality in 1978, and the attractions were obvious. For a price which included return ferry travel, plus the freedom to take your own car and all the baggage you

needed with no restrictions or surcharges, you could drive aboard in England, cross the Channel, drive off again in France rested, refreshed and well fed, and head for your chosen destination and self-catering accommodation at your own pace. A year later (1979), when the idea had proven its worth and popularity, self-drive holidays to Spain became another option.

The choice of holiday properties expanded rapidly, French gites and traditional Spanish casas in particular becoming (and remaining) hot favourites. The types of holidays on offer grew too to embrace options such as hotels, seaside apartments, cottages and villas, cabin cruisers, mobile homes, camping, family holidays and activity holidays – golf, touring, cycling and more.

In 1985 gite owners were encouraged by Brittany Ferries to place holiday journals in their properties so that departing guests could note recommendations to people following in their footsteps about where to go and what to see, such as local tourist attractions, markets, places to eat, 'hidden' beaches and beauty spots, and other useful and enlightening local knowledge. And such was the popularity of gites that the initial choice of just 15 soon grew to more than 1,500.

A particularly outstanding and ongoing success in the Brittany Ferries holidays story has been the Holiday France Direct service, whereby holidaymakers book with the property owners rather than through Brittany Ferries and benefit from discounted ferry travel.

By 2012 the huge and unstoppable advances in internet and website technology and instant, effortless communication had changed the way in which the majority of people choose and book a holiday. As a result, the dependence on traditional but increasingly expensive full-colour brochures has been reduced.

The selection of ferry-inclusive holidays, hotels, holiday properties and other accommodation offered by Brittany Ferries, and the administration of those bookings and associated services, remain important components in the company's long-term commitment to France – in particular the Channel and Atlantic coast regions and those which neighbour Brittany and Normandy – and to Spain's green northern provinces of Galicia, Asturias, Cantabria and, in the south-eastern corner of the Bay of Biscay, French-Spanish Basque country.

KEEPING THE FLEET AFLOAT

So what does it take, on a day-to-day, month-to-month, year-to-year basis, to operate Brittany Ferries' intensive schedules of frequent sailings, at the same time consistently achieving and maintaining the highest possible standards of safety and the quality of onboard services across the fleet?

The 'simple' answer, in round figures, is a staff of 2,500 men and women, of whom 1,700 are on the ships. Probing a little deeper, it quickly becomes apparent that the whole show can only achieve and sustain optimum performance, as it must, with the combined application of specialist expertise in many areas, both aboard and ashore.

The ships of Brittany Ferries operate in sophisticated international markets and are subject to not only the most rigorous safety standards but also to constantly-evolving legislation, consumer trends and methods of

Martine Jourdren (Group Managing Director & Chairman of Executive Board)

Christophe Mathieu (Group Strategy & Commercial Director)

Frédéric Pouget (Group Maritime Port & Operations Director)

communication. Hence a typical crew is the epitome of teamwork performing with clockwork precision, dealing on a daily basis with hundreds of complex demands, many of which are never apparent to passengers – which of course is how it should be.

Over 40 years Brittany Ferries has nurtured a unique and original service, business culture and identity. The company's major shareholders are those very same groundbreaking farming co-operatives which created the company in 1973 and which have remained faithful to its ethics and philosophy. The latest ships are the prodigies of Brittany Ferries' 'clean seas' policy,

running on low-sulphur fuels, producing significantly less CO2 than did their predecessors and utilising special paints which are friendly to the marine environment. In service, the *Armorique* and the *Pont-Aven* monitor the quality of seawater and the data is relayed to scientists ashore.

Brittany Ferries also sustains its long-standing partnerships in important international marine environmental projects, working in recent years alongside scientists from organisations such as Oceanopolis, Roscoff Biological Station and British-based charity ORCA, the latter dedicated to furthering

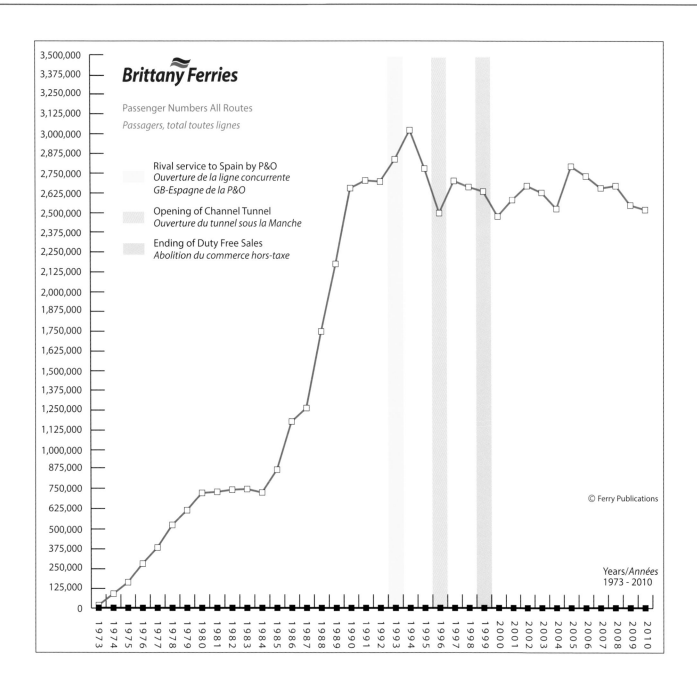

Brittany Ferries

Passenger Numbers All Routes
Passagers, total toutes lignes

Rival service to Spain by P&O
*Ouverture de la ligne concurrente
GB-Espagne de la P&O*

Opening of Channel Tunnel
Ouverture du tunnel sous la Manche

Ending of Duty Free Sales
Abolition du commerce hors-taxe

© Ferry Publications

Years/*Années*
1973 - 2010

Mont St Michel
(Brittany Ferries).

the knowledge, understanding and preservation of marine mammals prevalent in Channel waters.

WHO STEERS THE SHIP

Brittany Ferries is managed by an executive board, based at company headquarters in Roscoff, whose members are Martine Jourdren (Group Managing Director and Finance Director), Christophe Mathieu (Group Strategy & Commercial Director) and Frédéric Pouget (Port & Operations Director). Jean-Marc Roué is company President and Jean-François Jacob is the Vice President.

CHAPTER NINE

The image of consistency

Over 40 years Brittany Ferries has developed a brand identity which is distinctive, memorable and instantly recognisable wherever you see it – adorning a holiday brochure, colour advertisement, TV commercial, email, website, terminal building or the exterior of any ship in the fleet.

The company's logo is the result of a continuous process of evolution, rather than revolution, in graphic design. It's a signature which guarantees to customers that in return for their hard-earned cash they will experience the very best of the long-established core values of the Brittany Ferries travel experience – comfort, style, service, French cuisine, money-saving boutique shopping and more – and when applied to Brittany Ferries holidays gives the further reassurance of quality accommodation in desirable locations throughout France and northern Spain.

In order to be credible, these promises of good things to come need to be presented to their respective target audiences in ways which are consistent and lacking any possible ambiguity. Hence the need for corporate identity guidelines, imposing strict rules on the ways in which every form of communication and badging is presented

Brittany Ferries

France & Spain
Golf breaks

2013

Unbeatable value • unrivalled service • superb courses for *any* golf lover

LE RESTAURANT

COCKTAILS

Le cocktail du jour / Cocktail of the day .... £ 3.95 0.00 €uros
Mojito .... £ 3.95 0.00 €uros
Bacardi Superior, lemon juice, mint leaf, sugar, soda
Red apple martini .... £ 3.95 0.00 €uros
Bacardi Superior, lemon juice, mint leaf, sugar, soda
Piña Colada .... £ 3.95 0.00 €uros
Bacardi Superior & Dark rum, pineapple juice, coconut milk
Long Island iced tea .... £ 3.95 0.00 €uros
Gin, Vodka, Cointreau, Dark rum, lemon juice, Coca-Cola
Sex on the beach .... £ 3.95 0.00 €uros
Vodka Smirnoff, Malibu, Manzana verde, orange and cranberry juice
Margarita .... £ 3.95 0.00 €uros
Tequila, Cointreau, lemon juice
Irish Coffee .... £ 3.95 0.00 €uros
Whisky Jameson, coffee, sugar and cream

COCKTAILS SANS ALCOOL / ALCOHOL FREE

Bora Bora .... £ 2.20 0.00 €uros
Orange, pineapple and guava juice with a dash of vanilla
The Pink Panther .... £ 3.95 0.00 €uros
Pineapple and guava juice, coconut milk, grenadine and caramel syrup

COGNAC   Single 2cl

Courvoisier VS .... £ 2.30 0.00 €uros
Rémy Martin VSOP .... £ 2.90 0.00 €uros

CALVADOS, ARMAGNAC

Calvados Boulard Grand Solage ...... £ 2.20 0.00 €uros
Armagnac Dupeyron VSOP .... £ 2.90 0.00 €uros

LIQUEURS

Malibu, Manzana verde ....
Pippermint, Baileys Original Irish cream ....
Cointreau, Tia Maria, Southern Confort ....

WINE (AOC)

Cellier des Dauphins (white, rose or red) ....

Blanc / White   10 cl

Kir Muscadet blackcurrant liqueur .... £ 2.00 0.00 €uros
Muscadet .... £ 1.90 0.00 €uros
Sèvre et Maine sur Loire - Organic
Sancerre Domaine Salmon Sauvignon ....
Bourgogne Chardonnay Tête de cuvée M. Laroche ...
Chablis Billaud Simon Chardonnay ....

Rosé / Rose

Cabernet d'Anjou Leduc-Frouin ....
Côtes de Provence
Domaine Gavoty Cuvée Clarendon

Rouge / Red

Beaujolais Villages Château de la Pierre
Loron et Fils
Bordeaux Ch. Haut Canteloup
2007 1ère Côtes de Blaye
Bourgogne Pinot Noir 2009 Joseph Faiveley ....
Bordeaux Château Noaillac 2005/06
Cru Bourgeois du Médoc

CHAMPAGNE

Nicolas Feuillatte Brut ou/or Rose 20 cl
Laurent Perrier Brut .... 75 cl
Moët & Chandon Brut Impérial .... 75 cl
Veuve Clicquot Ponsardin .... 75 cl
Carte Jaune Brut

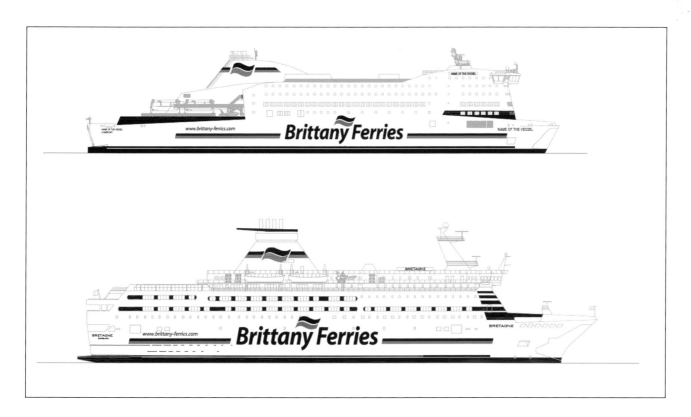

to customers and prospects.

These guidelines embrace everything from the specific palette choices guaranteeing accurate representation of the blue and red in the company logo to typography in its various forms and the use of approved photographs and other images. Faithfully reproducing the colours of the company logo is a challenge which has to embrace the fact that when applied to the ships in the fleet, and is very visible by its size, the logo is constantly exposed to salt spray and all weathers and demands the application of specialist and highly resilient marine paint produced to achieve, as close as is possible, identical colour matches.

The logo is the masthead of Brittany Ferries' corporate identity and as the company has developed new and additional services and products over the years, notably holidays, the logo has been adapted to promote them and to address specific target markets such as freight operators and group travel.

The strict adherence to these corporate guidelines has a further major benefit, albeit to the company itself: the accumulative effect of consistency is to reinforce the brand values at every opportunity, thereby achieving maximum value for money from the annual marketing budget.

Cap Finistére *(FotoFlite)*

The Fleet/la Flotte

ARMORIQUE

Launched	2009	Construction	2009
Gross tonnage	29,500	Jauge brute	29,500
Length	168.3m	Longueur	168.3m
Beam	26.8m	Largeur	26.8m
Maximum draught	6.5m	Tirant d'eau maxi	6.5m
Service speed	24 knots	Vitesse	24 nœuds
Crew	106	Equipage	106
Cars	470	Capacité garage	470
Passenger capacity	1,500	Capacité passagers	1,500

BARFLEUR

Launched	1992	Construction	1992
Gross tonnage	20,133	Jauge brute	20,133
Length	158.0m	Longueur	158.0m
Beam	23.30m	Largeur	23.30m
Maximum draught	5.40m	Tirant d'eau maxi	5.40m
Service speed	19.3 knots	Vitesse	19.3 nœuds
Crew	50	Equipage	50
Cars	590	Capacité garage	590
Passenger capacity	1,200	Capacité passagers	1,200

BRETAGNE

Launched	1989	Construction	1989
Gross tonnage	24,534	Jauge brute	24,534
Length	151m	Longueur	151m
Beam	26m	Largeur	26m
Maximum draught	6.20m	Tirant d'eau maxi	6.20m
Service speed	21 knots	Vitesse	21 noeuds
Crew	130	Equipage	130
Cars	580	Capacité garage	580
Passenger capacity	2,056	Capacité passagers	2,056

CAP FINISTERE

Launched	2001	Construction	2001
Gross tonnage	32,728	Jauge brute	32,728
Length	204m	Longueur	204m
Beam	25m	Largeur	25m
Maximum draught	6.4m	Tirant d'eau maximum	6.4m
Service speed	28 knots	Vitesse	28 noeuds
Crew	107	Equipage	107
Cars		Capacité voitures	
/Freight	500 or 110	/Fret	500 ou 110
Passenger capacity	1,500	Capacité passagers	1,500

MONT ST MICHEL

Launched	2002	Construction	2002
Gross tonnage	35,586	Jauge brute	34,000
Length	173m	Longueur	173m
Beam	28.5m	Largeur	28.5m
Maximum draught	6.2m	Tirant d'eau maxi	6.2m
Service speed	21 knots	Vitesse	21 noeuds
Crew	135	Equipage	135
Cars	830	Capacité garage	830
Passenger capacity	2,170	Capacité passagers	2,170

NORMANDIE

Launched	1992	Construction	1992
Gross tonnage	27,541	Jauge brute	27,541
Length	161m	Longueur	161m
Beam	26m	Largeur	26m
Maximum draught	6m	Tirant d'eau maxi	6m
Service speed	20.5 knots	Vitesse	20.5 noeuds
Crew	137	Equipage	137
Cars	648	Capacité garage	648
Passenger capacity	2,100	Capacité passagers	2,100

The Fleet/la Flotte

The Fleet/la Flotte

NORMANDIE EXPRESS

Launched	2000	Construction	2000
Gross tonnage	6,581	Jauge brute	6,581
Length	97.2m	Longueur	97.2m
Beam	26.6m	Largeur	26.6m
Maximum draught	3.43m	Tirant d'eau maxi	6m
Service speed	42 Knots	Vitesse	42 Noeuds
Cars	280	Capacité garage	280
Passenger capacity	900	Capacité passagers	900

PONT-AVEN

Launched	2004	Construction	2004
Gross tonnage	41,000	Jauge brute	41,000
Length	185m	Longueur	185m
Beam	31m	Largeur	31m
Maximum draught	6.8m	Tirant d'eau maximum	6.8m
Service speed	27 Knots	Vitesse	27 Noeuds
Crew	184	Equipage	184
Cars	650	Capacité voitures	650
Passenger capacity	2,400	Capacité passagers	2,400

COTENTIN

Launched	2007	Construction	2007
Gross tonnage	25,000	Jauge brute	25,000
Length	167m	Longueur	167m
Beam	26.80m	Largeur	26.80m
Maximum draught	6.2m	Tirant d'eau maximum	6.2m
Service speed	24.5 Knots	Vitesse	24.5 Noeuds
Crew	50x	Equipage	50
Lorries	120	Capacité remorques	120
Passenger capacity	160	Capacité passagers	160